D1175973

PIONEERS OF WOMEN'S EDUCATION
IN THE UNITED STATES

PIONEERS
OF WOMEN'S EDUCATION IN
THE UNITED STATES

Emma Willard   Catherine Beecher
Mary Lyon

Edited By

WILLYSTINE GOODSELL

AMS PRESS
NEW YORK

Reprinted from the edition of 1931, New York
First AMS EDITION published 1970
Manufactured in the United States of America

International Standard Book Number: 0-404-02864-0

Library of Congress Card Catalog Number: 78-121279

AMS PRESS, INC.
NEW YORK, N.Y. 10003

PREFACE

This book attempts to fill an existing need for an account of the part played in the historical development of American education by certain outstanding women. The biographies of these pioneers are recounted rather fully and the more significant of their writings, already becoming rare, have been brought together in convenient form. It is to be hoped that instructors of the history of education will continue and extend a practice, here and there begun, of devoting some consideration to the material question of the education of women in bygone times and to the signal services rendered by women to the improvement of that education.

WILLYSTINE GOODSELL.

COLUMBIA UNIVERSITY,
NEW YORK CITY,
April, 1931.

CONTENTS

PART I

EMMA WILLARD

PART II

CATHERINE BEECHER

CONTENTS

PART III

MARY LYON

WOMEN'S EDUCATION IN AMERICA
BEFORE 1820

WHEN the English colonists settled in America they brought with them, naturally enough, the traditions and customs of the mother country respecting the status and education of women. Hence it followed that in the American colonies married women had no legal status, having surrendered their legal personality to their husbands at marriage. In the words of the old English common law, "husband and wife are one and the husband is the one." When a married woman was involved in legal difficulties, her husband represented her in the courts. Because a married woman (and most women *were* married) was not an independent person in the eyes of the law she could not make a will or enter into a contract or bring suit for the protection of her interests. All these rights were vested in her husband who also had by law sole rights of guardianship of the children.

1

Not only was the legal status of married women a nullity but their economic position was markedly inferior. At marriage a woman surrendered all right to administer her property, both real and personal, into the hands of her husband who enjoyed the income thereof without being compelled by law to give an account of his stewardship. With the exception of her personal clothing a husband owned all his wife's property and could squander it or use it to pay his debts. Such was the common law of England and so it was in the American colonies and in all but a handful of the states of the American Union up to the Civil War.

In regard to the education deemed suitable for women, the colonists were likewise swayed by English traditions. Everywhere it was held that woman's sphere was in the home, bearing and rearing "a quiver full" of children to people the virgin wilderness, and carrying on a varied round of domestic industries without which the colonists could not have survived the rigors and deprivations of their new environment. From dawn to dark girls and women were employed in the preparation and preservation of food, in spinning, carding, weaving, fashioning garments, brewing ale and medicines and carrying on a dozen other pursuits by which the household was maintained. Every good home was a training school in which daughters were instructed by their mothers in the domestic occupations that these young women would some day be called upon to perform in their own homes.

Under these conditions it was accepted without challenge that, since women would do little of the world's work requiring book knowledge, their intellectual education could quite properly be neglected or reduced to a meager minimum. Moreover there is ample evidence that the intellectual abilities of women were generally believed to be inferior if not actually nonexistent. The Puritan colonists of Massachusetts Bay and Connecticut looked with scant favor on intellectual pursuits for girls. Witness the comments of Governor Winthrop with respect to Mistress Hopkins, the studious wife of the governor of Hartford colony. In his Journal, under the date 1645, Governor Winthrop sets down that this unfortunate lady had "fallen into a sad infirmity, the loss of her understanding and reason . . . by occasion of her giving herself wholly to reading and writing, and had written many books."

Too late, if we may believe the chronicler, had her husband seen "his error." "For if she had attended her household affairs, and such things as belonged to women, and had not gone out of her way and calling to meddle in such things as are proper for men, whose minds are stronger, etc., she had kept her wits, and might have improved them usefully and honorably in the place God had set her."

Even as late as 1778 Abigail Adams writes her husband John Adams, then sitting with the Continental Congress: "But in this country, you need not be told how much female education is neglected, nor how fashionable it has been to ridicule female learning: though I acknowledge it my happiness to be connected with a person of a more generous mind and liberal sentiments."

Yet it would be a mistake to assert that girls were given no schooling in the struggling colonies that dotted the coast from Massachusetts Bay to the Carolinas. Quite commonly little girls attended the "dame schools" in the New England and Middle colonies. Here they learned the rudiments of reading and sometimes writing (almost never arithmetic), how to recite the Lord's Prayer and parts of the Westminster Catechism, and how to drop a curtsey to their elders and betters. In 1647 the colony of Massachusetts Bay, and three years later its sister colony, Connecticut, had enacted laws requiring towns of fifty families to provide elementary schools and towns of one hundred families Latin grammar schools in order that "learning may not be buried in the graves of our forefathers." Under difficulties, and with numerous lapses, the New England towns did provide these schools and managed to pay the schoolmaster's meager salary from public funds. But girls were almost universally excluded from the town elementary schools until after the Revolutionary War. A few exceptions exist. During the later eighteenth century some towns permitted girls to have an hour or two of instruction during the morning hours from five to seven when boys were not using the school building. Also the colony of Connecticut opened its elementary schools to girls in 1771. Two years later the town of Portsmouth, New Hampshire, invited one David McClure "to take care of a public school of

Misses." In his diary the master records it as his belief that "This is . . . the only female School (supported by the town) in New England, it is a wise and useful institution."

In the Dutch colony of New Netherlands, where parish elementary schools were established in compliance with the provisions of the Synod of Dort, it is probable that girls were admitted to learn the elements of reading and writing early in the history of the colony. There is no explicit statement to this effect, however, prior to 1733. Small provision was made in the Middle and Southern colonies for the elementary education of girls of the poorer class, other than a few parochial and charity schools. Southern girls in the families of well-to-do planters were quite commonly instructed in their homes by tutors and then sent to England to "finish" a dubious education. One of these tutors, a young Princeton graduate named Philip Fithian, records in his journal in 1773 an account of the studies pursued by the five daughters of Mr. Robert Carter of Virginia. The eldest, named Priscilla, a girl of sixteen, was reading Addison's *Spectator,* writing and "beginning to Cypher," while the youngest was "beginning her letters." Evidently the instruction given these girls did not go far beyond the work of the primary school of our own day.

During the eighteenth century there was imported into the colonies from England a new type of school—the private day or boarding school. Colonial newspapers contain numerous advertisements of such schools not unlike the following from the *New York Gazetteer* of April 7, 1774: "J. and M. Tanner inform the public that they intend moving to another residence where they will set up a boarding school for young ladies." Not only do they propose to teach "Reading, after the rules of the best grammarians, . . . Writing, in all the useful and ornamental hands; . . . Arithmetic . . . *by a method adapted to their capacities . . .*"[1] but they add "Needlework of all Kinds, Music, dancing, drawing, French, tambour work and every polite accomplishment. . . ." All are to be taught by a method "similar to that of the most approved English Boarding Schools."

Here, then, is clear evidence that the boarding school of the mother country, with all its emphasis on showy

[1] Italics mine.

7

accomplishments and its lamentable lack of sound instruction on subjects requiring thought and judgment has been transplanted to colonial soil. These establishments, together with similar private day schools and an occasional night school to which women were admitted, furnished the sole means of "higher" education for well-to-do girls prior to the Revolution. Since the fees of these schools were not low according to colonial standards, the rank and file of girls must have received little more instruction than was furnished by the dame schools—if they were not wholly illiterate.

After the six devastating years of the War for Independence, the citizens of the thirteen original colonies, now free and independent states, set their faces hopefully toward the future. Gradually the popular democratic doctrines of liberty and equality, long restricted to men, began to be applied to women and their education. In the New England states the town elementary schools were very generally opened to girls during the decades succeeding the war. Moreover there sprang up in all the states a novel type of secondary school—the academy or "female seminary" for girls. To be sure a few of these institutions, e. g., the Moravian Academy at Bethlehem, Pennsylvania, had been founded before the Revolution. But after 1782 these schools sprang up like mushroom growths from Maine to Georgia and as far west as frontier towns had been pushed. There can be little doubt that the "female seminaries" in which our great-grandmothers and grandmothers were educated represented, at least in many instances, an improvement over the education furnished in the private day and boarding schools of an earlier period. Noah Webster, in 1806, refers to "two distinguished schools for young ladies" in Connecticut—the Union School in New Haven and the Academy in Litchfield which later achieved considerable renown. These academies, Webster tells us, taught primary branches, geography, grammar, the languages, and higher branches of mathematics. Philadelphia boasted an academy "for the instruction of Young Ladies" as early as 1787, in which Mr. John Poor taught the three R's, "English Grammar, Composition, Rhetoric and Geography."

Some of the academies in which women were instructed were incorporated schools, like Mr. Poor's academy, which proudly claimed to be the first "Female Academy, established by a Charter of Incorporation . . . in the United States, and perhaps in the world. . . ." One of the first chartered academies open to girls in Massachusetts was Bradford, founded in 1803 as a co-educational school, but in 1836 changed to a seminary for girls. It was followed, before the lapse of a generation, by Byfield Academy (1818), Adams Academy, Derry, New Hampshire (1824), Ipswich Female Seminary (1828), Abbot Academy (1829), and Wheaton Seminary, Norton, Massachusetts (1834). In the Middle and Southern states academies also sprang up, some of which became renowned in their localities, as the academy for girls in Winston-Salem, North Carolina, founded by the Moravians in 1802, and Elizabeth Academy in Mississippi, established in 1817 and proudly claiming to be of collegiate grade.

But there is a darker aspect of the educational picture which must not be overlooked. Despite the fact that not a few incorporated academies were in existence in 1815, which offered to young women the opportunity to secure a more solid education than ever before, these schools were usually not free and were scattered over a wide area. In consequence girls of the poorer class were quite generally excluded from the academies, and prosperous parents, who were willing to send their daughters to perhaps distant towns to secure an education, were chiefly the patrons of the new institutions. Side by side with the better academies there sprang up a weedy growth of private "female seminaries," meagerly financed, meagerly staffed and equipped, offering a course of study taught by ill-educated women which was little if any superior to the private day and boarding schools of the eighteenth century. It is these schools that Emma Willard and Catherine Beecher so vigorously attacked in their writings. They were well acquainted with them and clearly understood the flimsy economic substructure on which these institutions were reared, as well as the superficial attainments of their "mistresses" and teachers. Writing of the causes of the failure of the Hartford Seminary, after she had severed her connection with it in 1833, Catherine Beecher says:

"The decline of Hartford Seminary after I left was the necessary result of want of endowment. . . . Had [it] been endowed with only half the funds bestowed on our poorest colleges for young men, and the college plan of divided responsibilities thus been made permanent, most of my best teachers would have been retained, or, if removed at diverse intervals, their places would have been supplied by the highest class of teachers, as are college professorships." She adds that "no library or apparatus was provided, nor could the limited income from my tuition fees secure them." [1]

This, then, was the educational situation when Emma Willard came upon the scene about 1807. Most states in New England were offering free elementary education to girls in town schools. Here and there in all the states were academies fairly well endowed, sometimes chartered by the state, and in a few instances open to girls. Everywhere were springing up "female seminaries," founded by indigent women of scanty education, who were exploiting the girls attending their schools in a desperate attempt to make a "genteel" living. The day of the free public high school had not yet dawned; and college education of women was unheard of.

[1] BARNARD, HENRY, *American Journal of Education,* Vol. 28, p. 82, January, 1877.

PART I

EMMA WILLARD

Life of Emma Willard.
Selections from her "Plan for Improving Female Education."
Selections from her Textbooks.

EMMA WILLARD

(Facing page 14)

EMMA WILLARD, EDUCATOR AND BUILDER

SIXTY years have passed since the death of Emma Willard and it is now possible to view in true perspective the services rendered by this gifted and strong-hearted pioneer to the education of women. The enthusiastic judgment of Thomas Wentworth Higginson [1] that, in publishing her "Plan for Improving Female Education" in 1819 and in establishing at Waterford a school under (partial) patronage of the state, Emma Willard "laid the foundation upon which every woman's college or coeducational college may be said to rest" is probably somewhat of an overstatement. Yet the passage of time has served to brighten rather than dim the achievements of this educational reformer and to reveal her as a vitalizing influence, a veritable builder of the solid base of a new education for women upon which subsequent leaders could rear a superstructure. In this day, when equality of educational opportunity for women is

[1] In an article in *Harper's Bazaar,* 1893.

almost a commonplace, no one can read of the passionate desire of Emma Willard to secure justice for her sex in education, her wide-visioned plan for the reconstruction of the pseudo-education accorded to girls, her never-swerving faith in the possibilities of women, and the courageous, unceasing efforts she put forth to realize her dreams, without a genuine thrill of admiration. This woman was in very truth a crusader in a great cause, to whom American women owe in measurable degree their rich educational opportunities.

Of good New England stock, Emma Willard was born in the village of Berlin, Connecticut, February 23, 1787. She was the daughter of Captain Samuel Hart and Lydia Hinsdale Hart, his second wife, and was the sixteenth child of a family of seventeen. Her father is described as a man of scholarly tastes, who represented his town in the General Court at Hartford. He was descended on the mother's side from the Rev. Thomas Hooker, able leader of the Hartford colony in the early days. Emma's mother was a descendant of Rev. Theodore Hinsdale of Massachusetts, for whom the town of Hinsdale was named.

Within the large circle of her family the girl Emma

grew up, attending the public school of the village and early showing herself an eager and enthusiastic student. In the long winter evenings Captain Hart read aloud to his family from Gibbon's *History of Rome, Paradise Lost,* and *The Spectator.* When she was fifteen years old Emma went to the town academy, incorporated by the General Assembly, where for two years she studied under the able guidance of one Thomas Miner, a Yale graduate and later a distinguished physician.

At the early age of seventeen the professional career of Emma Hart began, when she was appointed "mistress" of the district school of Kensington, which was in session only during the summer. Here she soon revealed that natural gift for teaching which distinguished her throughout her academic life and did not escape the notice of the townspeople. Her brothers, sympathizing with their sister's zest for knowledge, assisted her to meet the expenses of a winter's study in the school of the Patten sisters in Hartford and later in the celebrated school of Mrs. Royse, where young ladies were taught the three R's, geography, French, drawing, painting, and needlework. In 1806 she was offered a position in the Academy of Berlin, where so recently she had been a student. Once more she made a pronounced success as a teacher and the next year received no less than three offers to teach outside the state—in Westfield, Massachusetts, in Hudson, New York, and in Middlebury, Vermont. She chose to go to Westfield, where an academy for girls had been established in 1800 which had already achieved a good reputation. Here again she added to her laurels as a teacher and "female assistant." A few months later Middlebury made her a tempting offer to assume the management of the "female academy" there, an offer which she finally accepted with the reluctant consent of the Westfield authorities.

At this time Middlebury was a quiet, dignified college town of conservative traditions. Its society included several graduates of Yale, Dartmouth, and other New England colleges. The new head of the academy was welcomed into the somewhat exclusive circle of Middlebury's intellectual élite and soon became acquainted with the president of the college, Dr. Henry Davis, and the founder of the academy, Hon. Horatio Seymour. Her association with the educated group of townspeople, who formed a little aristocracy, soon led her to perceive that these men did not take the education of girls very seriously. Girls, to be sure, were to be introduced to various fields of knowledge and permitted to make their bow, but a long and thorough acquaintanceship with learning was reserved for men. The prevailing attitude of men toward the education of their daughters is exemplified by the fact that the grave dons of Middlebury College not infrequently attended the interesting examinations and closing exercises of the "female academy," on the invitation of its head, but never once reciprocated the courtesy by inviting academy members to the sacrosanct commencement exercises at Middlebury College.

There can be no doubt that a growing realization of the true state of affairs with respect to women's education led Emma Willard to form some years later the ardent resolution that was to be the dominating purpose of her life—the determination to secure for her sex full opportunities for learning as a human right and to extend these privileges so far as possible to all women. In this purpose she never weakened during the whole of her long and useful life and to it she dedicated all her remarkable intellectual powers and all the energy, initiative, and persistence of a vigorous personality.

In 1809 Miss Hart married Dr. John Willard, who had given up his medical practice to accept the post of Marshal of Vermont, tendered him in 1801 by President Jefferson. After her marriage Emma Willard not only carried on a variety of pursuits connected with the house and farm but found time to satisfy her hunger for knowledge by reading her husband's medical books, studying geometry with his nephew, reading Locke's *Essay on the Human Understanding,* and Paley's popular *Moral Philosophy.* In 1812 serious financial reverses came to Dr. Willard which greatly crippled his income. This was his wife's opportunity, not alone to recoup the family fortunes but to attempt the improvement of women's education. In 1814, with her husband's sympathetic help and counsel, she opened a boarding school for girls. Referring to her motives in taking this step Mrs. Willard wrote:

"When I began my boarding school in Middlebury my leading motive was to relieve my husband from financial difficulties. I had also the further motive of keeping a better school than those about me; but it was not till a year or two after that I formed the design of effecting an important change in education by the introduction of a grade of schools for women higher than any heretofore known. My neighborhood to Middlebury College made me feel bitterly the disparity in educational facilities between the two sexes, and I hoped that if the matter was once set before the men as legislators, they would be ready to correct the error."

The new school soon met with the success that crowned all of Emma Willard's serious efforts, and before long at least seventy girls were enrolled. The course of study was enriched by new subjects as fast as Mrs. Willard herself could learn them, and methods of instruction were constantly improved. But during this busy period Mrs. Willard did not lose sight of her half-formed plan to appeal to the legislature for financial aid in putting the education of women on a higher plane. Many were the consultations held with her liberal-minded husband on this subject and it was a great joy to her that he encouraged and actively aided her in realizing her purpose. For several years she worked away on her *Plan for Improving Female Education,* shaping and reshaping her arguments to make them cogent and persuasive. During this period she writes: "I determined to inform myself and increase my personal influence and fame as a teacher, calculating that in this way I might be sought for in other places, where influential men would carry my project before some legislature, for the sake of obtaining a good school." [1]

Because of the fact that five pupils from Waterford, New York, were attending her school, Mrs. Willard turned her eyes toward the prosperous state of New York and dreamed of a seminary for girls in the Hudson Valley. Through her Waterford pupils she came to know General Van Schoonhoven, who was deeply interested in her *Plan* and offered to bring it to the attention of Governor De Witt Clinton of New York. Gladly complying with this suggestion, Mrs. Willard sent her precious manuscript to Governor Clinton with an explanatory letter, both written in the beautiful, legible script of which she was justly proud. After months of delay came the eagerly awaited reply of the governor in which he declared that he had read her "manuscript

---

[1] Quoted in LUTZ, *Emma Willard, Daughter of Democracy,* p. 61, Houghton Mifflin Co., Boston, 1929.

with equal pleasure and instruction" and added these encouraging words:

"I shall be gratified to see this work in print, and still
more pleased to see you at the head of the proposed institution, enlightening it by your talents, guiding it by
your experience, and practically illustrating its merits
and its blessings." [1]

On the advice of their friends in Waterford, Dr. and
Mrs. Willard spent some weeks in Albany during the
legislative session of 1819. At the request of various
members of the legislature, Mrs. Willard read to them
the manuscript of her *Plan;* and, despite the conven-
tions of the age relegating women strictly to private life,
she impressed these men very favorably by her public-
spirited enthusiasm for the cause of women's education.
Yet in the end the legislature did relatively little to enable Mrs. Willard to realize her dream of a higher school
for girls adequately endowed from public funds. To be
sure an act was passed granting a charter to the "Waterford Academy for Young Ladies," which she was urged
to administer, and including that institution in the list
of schools to receive financial aid from the state "literary

[1] Quoted in Lutz, *op. cit.,* pp. 63, 64.

fund." But the recommendation of a committee that the projected Waterford Academy be given an endowment of five thousand dollars received an adverse vote by the legislature.

Returning to Middlebury with her hopes somewhat dimmed, Mrs. Willard published her *Plan* in pamphlet form at her own expense under the title *An Address to the Public; Particularly to the Members of the Legislature of New York Proposing a Plan for the Improvement of Female Education.* It was widely read both in America and in Europe and stirred general interest and approval. The clarity and persuasive logic of her appeal, its sanity and freedom from bitterness won for it a favorable hearing from many liberal-minded men. President Monroe and Thomas Jefferson are said to have approved it and John Adams, who had always encouraged his talented wife Abigail in her studies, wrote Mrs. Willard a cordial letter of commendation.[1] Of course the *Plan* was too unconventional and daring not to arouse opposition among conservatives. The conviction that women's work was wholly in the home, making pies and darning socks, was too deeply grounded to be

[1] See LUTZ, *op. cit.,* p. 66.

uprooted all at once. Of what use was book-learning to women? Would it make them better cooks and seam-stresses, better nurses of the sick and caretakers of chil-dren? Above all would not the higher education of women tend to make them ambitious and thus upset the established order? Thus it happened to Emma Wil-lard, as to every other reformer in social history, that she won the plaudits and help of the few, the ridicule and sneers of those who feared social change, and the indifference of the many who regarded the *Plan* as too far in advance of public opinion to accomplish impor-tant results.

In the spring of 1819 Mrs. Willard removed her school from Middlebury to Waterford, New York. The citi-zens of the town had appointed a board of trustees who had leased a large three-story building known as the "Mansion House" to serve as the home of the new academy. As yet the New York Legislature had given no financial aid to the school but Mrs. Willard attacked her new venture in sturdy hope of such assistance. A year later Governor Clinton once more appealed to the leg-islature in behalf of the academy, reminding its mem-bers that the new school represented "the only attempt ever made in this country to promote the education of the female sex by the patronage of government" and urging them not to be "deterred by common-place ridicule from extending their munificence to this meritorious institution." Unfortunately this appeal, however sincere and urgent, could not weaken the entrenched prejudice of the legislators against the education of women. A bill granting two thousand dollars to the school passed the senate but was voted down in the assembly. Furthermore the regents of the University of the State of New York decided to withhold from the academy all assistance from the state "literary fund."

It is not difficult to imagine Mrs. Willard's bitter disappointment and dismay at this failure of her plans. She tells us that she felt the humiliating defeat of all her hopes "almost to frenzy" and years afterward could not recall it "without agitation." But out of her utter disillusionment with the Albany politicians was born the resolve that her cause should be brought before the people who, when they were convinced of the justice of a more generous education for women, would bring the pressure of an enlightened public opinion to bear upon recalcitrant legislators.

Help and encouragement were to come to this daunt-less pioneer sooner than she expected. Certain prominent citizens of Troy invited her to move her school to that city, with the promise of financial assistance. On March 26, 1821, the Common Council of Troy passed a resolu-tion to raise four thousand dollars by special tax for the purchase of a building suitable for a female academy. The next month a three-story wooden building known as "Moulton's Coffee House" was purchased and addi-tional funds were raised by subscription to be expended in repairs. A board of trustees was then appointed by the council and, with exemplary wisdom, these gentle-men in turn appointed an advisory committee of women to confer with Mrs. Willard from time to time on im-portant matters concerning the school. In this way the active interest of a body of influential women was secured for the new experiment.

In that same spring of 1821 Mrs. Willard moved her school from Waterford to Troy, although she was obliged to find temporary accommodations until the school building, repaired and furnished in accordance with her suggestions, was ready for occupancy in the autumn. When the new school threw open its doors in

September, there flocked through them ninety young women representing seven states as widely scattered as Vermont, Georgia, and Ohio. Alma Lutz thus describes the beginning of this hopeful educational experiment:

"Mrs. Willard was thirty-four years old when she opened her school in Troy and embarked upon a venture which no woman before had tried. Beautiful, vigorous, earnest, and highly intellectual, she was eminently fitted for the task. Parents were favorably impressed by her charming manner and her ability. Pupils idealized her and were fired with ambition by her enthusiasm. The first years in Troy brought the annoyances, difficulties, and misrepresentations which usually attend every progressive enterprise, but these faded into insignificance as Mrs. Willard saw her school grow in numbers and in popular favor." [1]

When Mrs. Willard's enterprise is viewed from the standpoint of her cherished plan of state support for an advanced seminary for girls, these early years are seen to be full of disappointment. The New York Legislature turned a deaf ear to repeated pleas that the state give financial aid to the education of its daughters, as it had

[1] *Op. cit.,* p. 85.

long assisted the training of its sons. Fortunately the pronounced success of the school, not only in New York but in many other states, made public financial assistance less necessary with every year that passed and before long the seminary was on a sound economic basis.

Freed from anxiety on this score, Mrs. Willard was at liberty to attack the problem of an enrichment of the course of study. Little by little she added courses in algebra and geometry, history, geography, and natural philosophy (physics). No other girls' seminary in the country could boast all these "advanced" courses in the early twenties of the nineteenth century. In the teaching of geography by an appeal to the eye through charts and maps, Mrs. Willard seems to have been peculiarly successful. She was an intelligent student of the effects of her methods in developing her pupils' minds and she perceived that the classification of geographical facts on charts enabled the girls to grasp them more readily. With very little knowledge of psychology, but with abundant intelligence and zeal for the improvement of teaching, she hit upon objective methods of imparting knowledge which, in modified form, are in high esteem at present.

While in Waterford Mrs. Willard had been experimenting with improved methods of teaching geography, observing the results of these methods as she taught. The same experiments were carried on at Troy with such gratifying outcome that Mrs. Willard pushed forward the preparation of a geography textbook which should aid teachers in improving their instruction in this subject. About this time William C. Woodbridge was likewise engaged in writing a geography. Hearing of Mrs. Willard's book, then ready for publication, he got in ouch with her and discovered that her ideas and methods were quite similar to his own. The two authors thereupon decided to collaborate and published in 1822 their combined work, *A System of Universal Geography on the Principles of Comparison and Classification.* To this book, which won much favorable attention and a wide circulation, Mrs. Willard contributed the section on ancient geography together with an atlas, rules for constructing maps, and a set of problems on the globes. This was the first of a long list of publications by Mrs. Willard designed to improve methods of teaching not only geography—ancient and modern—but universal history, history of the United States, and morals. Among her well-known books were *History of the United States or Republic of America* (1829), *Willard's Historic Guide to the Temple of Time and Universal History for Schools* (1849), and *Morals for the Young* (1857).

Being a born executive, Mrs. Willard regulated her growing family of "young ladies" with moderation, common sense, and warm affection. Believing that school life should approximate life in the community and prepare for it, she organized a scheme of student self-government and appointed girls as monitors. These monitors made tours of inspection through the students' rooms and regularly reported cases of untidiness and infractions of discipline to the teacher who was officer of the week. The students were housed by twos in simple but comfortable rooms which they were expected to keep in perfect order. Each week one room-mate in turn had charge of the room and was held responsible for its cleanliness and for the tidiness of bureau drawers, which were duly inspected.

When questions of discipline arose, as of course they did, Mrs. Willard, instead of administering stern rebukes or condign punishment, summoned the offender to her room for a quiet talk. During the conversation she doubtless learned much of the temperament and difficulties of the girl and was able to render her real help in adapting herself more successfully to the demands of the school. With native psychological insight, Mrs. Willard not only sought to convince the culprit of her mistakes, but also to encourage her to improve her conduct by pointing out her good traits.

One of the greatest services which Emma Willard rendered to the education of her age was in training and sending out to the nation's newly established schools a corps of efficient teachers. Realizing very early in her career the crucial need of the country for trained teachers, she set out to supply that need by encouraging her girls to take up teaching as a profession. Furthermore she gave free tuition as a loan to promising young women who desired to become teachers but were too poor to meet the expenses of their education and training. It is said that during the seventeen years of her principalship of Troy Seminary she lent about seventy-five thousand dollars to needy girls who were fitting themselves to teach. Each young woman thus helped signed a contract to repay in time the money advanced for her education, in order that other girls might have a similar opportunity. Unfortunately little more than half ever repaid the loan. The young women who were graduated from Emma Willard's school, with a certificate signed by its famous principal, were equipped with the highest recommendation for a teaching position that the country offered prior to the founding of normal schools in 1837. In a very real sense Troy Female Seminary was a pioneer normal school, performing a conspicuous public service. Indeed, Mrs. Willard has stated that she sent forth from Troy two hundred trained teachers before one was graduated from a public normal school in this country.[1]

It would be pleasant to record that Mrs. Willard was as generously interested in the political enfranchisement of her sex as she was in their thorough education, but such seems not to have been the case. Imbued with the philosophy of her age that God had created men and women with different gifts and with sharply separated spheres of action, she actively discouraged her girls from becoming interested in politics—even in presidential elections. No doubt this able and farsighted general did not wish to imperil the cause of women's education—not yet won—by embroiling it with the dangerous young

[1] See Lutz, *op. cit.,* p. 98.

movement to secure the suffrage for women. Probably she was shrewd enough to perceive that the political emancipation of women must wait upon a slow and tedious change in public opinion, whereas the education of women was being steadily carried forward on a tide of popular favor. But even though the students of Mrs. Willard's life may understand her motives for keeping aloof from the suffrage movement, nevertheless lack of sympathy for its cause is disappointing to her admirers. Although she recognized, and even pointed out in an address on "The Advancement of Female Education" written in 1833, the many unjust discriminations against women in the existing laws, yet she seemed willing to leave their reform to the men "who regulate the law" and to the educated women of future generations.

During the years from 1821 to 1838, when Mrs. Willard was at the helm of Troy Seminary, it grew from a young and struggling institution into a famous school whose fine reputation spread not only throughout the United States but also in Europe. Daughters of several governors were educated there, as were the nieces of Washington Irving and the young niece of that courageous Mary Wollstonecraft of England, who first sounded the tocsin of woman's freedom in her *Vindication of the Rights of Woman*. In 1824 Lafayette visited the country he had helped to free and made a triumphal progress through the land. When Mrs. Willard heard that the hero was coming to Troy she invited him to visit the seminary. An arbor of evergreen had been constructed overnight in front of the school bearing the motto in flowers: "We owe our schools to freedom; freedom to Lafayette." Through this arbor came the distinguished visitor and was warmly welcomed by Mrs. Willard and her teachers, while the girl students, clad in white dresses and blue sashes, sang an ode to the national idol which had been written by Mrs. Willard in honor of the occasion. Lafayette seems to have been properly impressed both by the ode and by the school and when Mrs. Willard visited France some years later he returned her hospitable courtesies. Through his influence she was invited to court balls, visited the Chamber of Deputies, and was shown through the most famous French schools for girls.

A word should be said of the examination system in use for many years at Troy Seminary, a system which originated in Mrs. Willard's fruitful mind after she had

been denied admission to the examinations in Middlebury. Her plan was to hold examinations of her girls in
public and to invite professors of repute from various
institutions of learning to conduct the tests in the large
examination hall of the seminary. Bartlett quotes the
description of a former pupil of the interest evoked in
these examinations—hitherto unheard of for girls:

"Parents came from all quarters; the élite of Troy
and Albany assembled there. Principals from other
schools, distinguished legislators, and clergymen all came
to hear girls scan Latin verse, solve problems in Euclid,
go smoothly through fractions, and read their own
compositions in a promiscuous assemblage. A long line
of teachers anxiously awaited the calling of their classes;
and over all, our queenly Madam Willard presided with
royal grace and dignity." [1]

In 1832, after Greece had wrested its liberties from its
Turkish oppressor, Mrs. Willard became deeply interested in the improvement of the educational opportunities of the young women of Greece. Throwing herself
ardently into this cause, she sought by organizing meet-

---

[1] "Emma Willard, a Pioneer of Education for Women," *New
England Magazine,* p. 568, January, 1902.

ings and preparing addresses to arouse public interest in her plan for establishing a girls' school in Athens to train native teachers. Three of her addresses were published by the Troy Society and given a wide circulation. By her single-handed efforts Mrs. Willard raised three thousand dollars toward the founding of the school. Her campaign appears to have been an intensive one, for she wrote her sister that although the week's work she did in Troy was the heaviest in intellectual labor, it was "the happiest week I ever spent in Troy." The fortunate outcome of her efforts was the application of the funds she collected to the founding of a school in Athens for training women teachers.

In 1838, when Mrs. Willard was only fifty-one years of age, she retired from active management of the school at Troy, leaving its supervision to her son, John Willard, and his gifted wife, the latter having long been a successful teacher in the seminary. Under the able leadership of these two the school continued to grow in popular esteem and by 1850 was probably one of the finest girls' schools in the world, affording its students a broad and thorough education, approaching in its upper levels the work in colleges for men. Particularly advanced was the instruction in mathematics, astronomy, and mechanics. From 1847 to 1859 these subjects were taught by Miss Mary Hastings, a highly talented teacher, who used the textbooks employed at Yale in these studies. At a time when physics and chemistry were taught almost exclusively through textbooks in a purely theoretical way, Miss Hastings instructed her girls in chemistry by means of experiments, first performed by her and the next day by the students themselves.

After her retirement from Troy Seminary, its famous founder withdrew to Kensington, Connecticut, a parish of her native town of Berlin. At this time Henry Barnard was engaged in his memorable effort to improve the public schools of Connecticut and to advance educational methods in general. Into this work Mrs. Willard threw herself heart and soul, writing addresses and even accepting the superintendency of the four district schools of Kensington, in order that she might instruct the teachers in sounder educational practices. She had soon organized a group of young women, whom she called her normal pupils, and whom she instructed in better methods of teaching history and reading. To a few select spirits she also taught algebra and geometry.

From school to school she went, giving model lessons in reading, geography, and arithmetic. Having an abiding faith in the influence of women in the reform of education, Mrs. Willard aroused the women of Kensington to the need of the improvement of the public schools. Later she organized these housewives into the "Female Common School Association" which did effective work. In his reports to the state legislature, and in the school journal, Henry Barnard gave publicity to Mrs. Willard's methods of reform and these reports were copied and circulated in other states. It is little wonder that Emma Willard has been called "the apostle of normal schools."

After four years of arduous labor Mrs. Willard returned to Troy and soon was embarked in a strenuous campaign for the improvement of the schools of New York State. As the result of a ringing educational address published in the common school journals of the state, she was invited by the educational authorities to make a tour of several counties and address teachers' institutes. Setting out in her own carriage, with a former pupil at Troy as companion, she went from town to town speaking at institutes for teachers and pointing out the way of educational reform. Especially she urged the organization in every community of a committee of women to collaborate with the men in improving the training of teachers and methods of instruction. It is said that she traveled 700 miles on this educational crusade, instructing 500 teachers—men and women.

In the following year, 1846, Mrs. Willard made a more adventurous journey by stagecoach through the states of the West and South, addressing groups of teachers and citizens interested in education. Everywhere she met former Troy pupils, married and unmarried, and always they were proud and glad to entertain her. On this trip she covered 8,000 miles of territory, carrying her message of educational reform. In every town where she spoke she urged that women take an intelligent and active interest in the improvement of the common schools.

Mrs. Willard's second trip to Europe was made in 1854 on the occasion of the World's Educational Conference held in London. Here she renewed her acquaintance with Henry Barnard, who warmly greeted his former colleague and introduced her to outstanding educators from many lands. Her fame had preceded her and she received conspicuous attention, including a peeress's ticket to the House of Lords.

After her return to America Mrs. Willard made her home in a pleasant little house in the grounds of Troy Seminary, where she spent much time revising her many textbooks and influencing by her powerful, winning personality the many students who came to visit and drink tea with her. Busy with congenial literary work, she lived quietly and happily near her son and his wife, in close touch with the famous school which she had founded. She died on April 15, 1870, when she was eighty-three years of age. After her death, educational journals and newspapers united to extol her remarkable work in behalf of education, especially the neglected education of women. Ironically enough, the New York Legislature, which had so frequently refused to assist her work with public grants, passed solemn resolutions in appreciation of her achievements.

To the public, Emma Willard is chiefly known as the founder of Troy Seminary for girls. But to the students of her remarkable life she is even more esteemed as a gallant laborer in behalf of equal educational opportunities for women to be achieved through public grants, of thorough preparation for teachers and of the improvement of instruction in the common schools. Eager of mind, rich in enthusiasms, gifted with beauty of face and majesty of bearing, Emma Willard represents "the grand type of school mistress," who was an inspiration to all associated with her, a type that seems all too rare in these days of mass education. Yet every age has its stirring causes and has need of the vision and courage, the persistence and effort in pursuit of ideal goals that characterized this pioneer in the field of women's education.

An

A D D R E S S
TO THE PUBLIC

particularly

TO THE MEMBERS OF THE
L E G I S L A T U R E

of

NEW-YORK

proposing

A   P L A N

for improving

FEMALE EDUCATION

═══════════

By Emma Willard

═══════════

Second edition

═══════════

Middlebury:
Printed by J. W. Copeland.
1819.

A PLAN FOR IMPROVING FEMALE EDUCATION

The following selection contains Emma Willard's famous *Plan for Improving Female Education* which she published in 1819 at her own expense, after she had returned from a visit to Albany. It was during this visit that Mrs. Willard read the manuscript of her *Plan* to several members of the New York Legislature at their request. The temperate spirit in which the appeal is written, the cogency of the arguments in behalf of women's education, the firmly knit organization of the address and its grasp of an important educational principle of the present day—public support of schools— make this *Plan* an important educational contribution.

———

The object of this Address, is to convince the public, that a reform, with respect to female education, is necessary; that it cannot be effected by individual exertion, but that it requires the aid of the legislature: and further, by shewing the justice, the policy, and the magnanimity of such an undertaking, to persuade that body, to endow a seminary for females, as the commencement of such reformation.

The idea of a college for males, will naturally be associated with that of a seminary, instituted and endowed by the public; and the absurdity of sending ladies to college, may, at first thought, strike every one, to whom this subject shall be proposed. I therefore hasten to observe, that the seminary here recommended, will be as different from those appropriated to the other sex, as the female character and duties are from the male. The business of the husbandman is not to waste his endeavors, in seeking to make his orchard attain the strength and majesty of his forest, but to rear each, to the perfection of its nature.

That the improvement of female education will be considered by our enlightened citizens as a subject of importance, the liberality with which they part with their property to educate their daughters, is a sufficient evidence; and why should they not, when assembled in the legislature, act in concert to effect a noble object, which, though dear to them individually, cannot be accomplished by their unconnected exertions.

If the improvement of the American female character, and that alone, could be effected by public liberality, employed in giving better means of instruction; such improvement of one half of society, and that half, which barbarous and despotic nations have ever degraded, would of itself be an object, worthy of the most liberal government on earth; but if the female character be raised, it must inevitably raise that of the other sex: and thus does the plan proposed, offer, as the object of legislative bounty, to elevate the whole character of the community.

As evidence, that this statement does not exaggerate the female influence in society, our sex need but be considered, in the single relation of mothers. In this character, we have the charge of the whole mass of individuals, who are to compose the succeeding generation; during that period of youth, when the pliant mind takes any direction, to which it is steadily guided by a forming hand. How important a power is given by this charge! yet, little do too many of my sex know how, either to appreciate or improve it. Unprovided with the means of acquiring that knowledge, which flows liberally to the other sex—having our time of education devoted to frivolous acquirements, how should we understand the nature of the mind, so as to be aware of the importance of those early impressions, which we make upon the minds of our children?—or how should we be able to form enlarged and correct views, either of the character, to which we ought to mould them, or of the means most proper to form them aright?

Considered in this point of view, were the interests of male education alone to be consulted, that of females becomes of sufficient importance to engage the public attention. Would we rear the human plant to its perfection, we must first fertilize the soil which produces it. If it acquire its first bent and texture upon a barren plain, it will avail comparatively little, should it be afterwards transplanted to a garden. . . .

DEFECTS IN THE PRESENT MODE OF FEMALE EDUCATION, AND THEIR CAUSES

Civilized nations have long since been convinced, that education, as it respects males, will not, like trade, regulate itself; and hence, they have made it a prime object to provide that sex with everything requisite to facilitate their progress in learning: but female education has been left to the mercy of private adventurers; and the consequence has been to our sex, the same, as it would have been to the other, had legislatures left their accommodations, and means of instruction, to chance also. . . .

Male education flourishes, because, from the guardian care of legislatures, the presidencies and professorships of our colleges, are some of the highest objects to which the eye of ambition is directed. Not so with female institutions. Preceptresses of these, are dependent on their pupils for support, and are consequently liable to become the victims of their caprice. In such a situation, it is not more desirable to be a preceptress, than it would be, to be a parent, invested with the care of children, and responsible for their behaviour, but yet, depending on them for subsistence, and destitute of power to enforce their obedience.

Feminine delicacy requires, that girls should be educated chiefly by their own sex. This is apparent from considerations, that regard their health and conveniences, the propriety of their dress and manners, and their domestic accomplishments.

Boarding schools, therefore, whatever may be their defects, furnish the best mode of education provided for females.

Concerning these schools it may be observed:

1. They are temporary institutions, formed by individuals, whose object is present emolument. But they cannot be expected to be greatly lucrative; therefore, the individuals who establish them, cannot afford to provide suitable accommodations, as to room. At night, the pupils are frequently crowded in their lodging rooms; and during the day, they are generally placed together in one apartment, where there is a heterogeneous mixture

of different kinds of business, accompanied with so much noise and confusion, as greatly to impede their progress in study.

2. As individuals cannot afford to provide suitable accommodations as to room, so neither can they afford libraries, and other apparatus, necessary to teach properly the various branches in which they pretend to instruct.

3. Neither can the individuals who establish these schools afford to provide suitable instruction. It not unfrequently happens, that one instructress teaches, at the same time, and in the same room, ten or twelve distinct branches. . . .

4. It is impossible, that in these schools such systems should be adopted and enforced, as are requisite for properly classing the pupils. Institutions for young gentlemen are founded by public authority, and are permanent; they are endowed with funds, and their instructors and overseers, are invested with authority to make such laws, as they shall deem most salutary. From their permanency, their laws and rules are well known. With their funds they procure libraries, philosophical apparatus, and other advantages, superior to what can elsewhere be found; and to enjoy these, individuals are placed under their discipline, who would not else be subjected to it. Hence the directors of these institutions

can enforce, among other regulations, those which enable them to make a perfect classification of their students. They regulate their qualifications for entrance, the kind and order of their studies, and the period of their remaining at the seminary. Female schools present the reverse of this. Wanting permanency, and dependent on individual patronage, had they the wisdom to make salutary regulations, they could neither enforce nor purchase compliance. The pupils are irregular in their times of entering and leaving school; and they are of various and dissimilar acquirements.

Each scholar, of mature age, thinks she has a right to judge for herself respecting what she is to be taught; and the parents of those, who are not, consider, that they have the same right to judge for them. Under such disadvantages, a school cannot be classed, except in a very imperfect manner.

5. It is for the interest of instructresses of boarding schools, to teach their pupils showy accomplishments, rather than those, which are solid and useful. Their object in teaching is generally present profit. In order to realize this, they must contrive to give immediate celebrity to their schools. If they attend chiefly to the cultivation of the mind, their work may not be manifest at the first glance; but let the pupil return home, laden with fashionable toys, and her young companions,

filled with envy and astonishment, are never satisfied till they are permitted to share the precious instruction. . . .

6. As these schools are private establishments, their preceptresses are not accountable to any particular persons. Any woman has a right to open a school in any place; and no one, either from law or custom, can prevent her. Hence the public are liable to be imposed upon, both with respect to the character and acquirements of preceptresses. I am far, however, from asserting that this is always the case. It has been before observed, that in the present state of things, the ordinary motives which actuate the human mind, would not induce ladies of the best and most cultivated talents, to engage in the business of instructing, from choice. But some have done it from necessity, and occasionally, an extraordinary female has occupied herself in instructing, because she felt that impulse to be active and useful, which is the characteristic of a vigorous and noble mind; and because she found few avenues to extensive usefulness open to her sex. But if such has been the fact, it has not been the consequence of any system, from which a similar result can be expected to recur with regularity; and it remains true, that the public are liable to imposition, both with regard to the character and acquirements of preceptresses. . . .

Those women, however, who deceive society as to the advantages which they give their pupils, are not charged with any ill intention. They teach as they were taught, and believe that the public are benefitted by their labours. Acquiring, in their youth, a high value for their own superficial accomplishments, they regard all others as supernumerary, if not unbecoming. Although these considerations exculpate individuals, yet they do not diminish the injury which society receives; for they show, that the worst which is to be expected from such instruction, is not that the pupils will remain ignorant; but that, by adopting the views of their teachers, they will have their minds barred against future improvement, by acquiring a disrelish, if not a contempt for useful knowledge.

7. Although, from a want of public support, preceptresses of boarding schools have not the means of enforcing such a system as would lead to a perfect classification of their pupils; and although they are confined in other respects within narrow limits, yet, because these establishments are not dependant [*sic*] on any public body, within those limits, they have a power far more arbitrary and uncontrolled, than is allowed the learned and judicious instructors of our male seminaries.

· · · · · · · · ·

Thus the writer has endeavoured to point out the defects of the present mode of female education; chiefly in order to show, that the great cause of these defects consists in a state of things, in which legislatures, under-valuing the importance of women in society, neglect to provide for their education, and suffer it to become the sport of adventurers for fortune, who may be both ignorant and vicious.

OF THE PRINCIPLES BY WHICH EDUCATION SHOULD BE REGULATED

To contemplate the principles which should regulate systems of instruction, and consider how little those principles have been regarded in educating our sex, will show the defects of female education in a still stronger point of light, and will also afford a standard, by which any plan for its improvement may be measured.

Education should seek to bring its subjects to the perfection of their moral, intellectual and physical nature: in order, that they may be of the greatest possible use to themselves and others: or, to use a different expression, that they may be the means of the greatest possible happiness of which they are capable, both as to what they enjoy, and what they communicate.

Those youth have the surest chance of enjoying and communicating happiness, who are best qualified, both by internal dispositions, and external habits, to perform with readiness, those duties, which their future life will most probably give them occasion to practice.

Studies and employments should, therefore, be selected, from one or both of the following considerations: either, because they are peculiarly fitted to improve the faculties; or, because they are such, as the pupil will most probably have occasion to practise in future life.

These are the principles, on which systems of male education are founded; but female education has not yet been systematized. Chance and confusion reign here. Not even is youth considered in our sex, as in the other, a season, which should be wholly devoted to improvement. Among families, so rich as to be entirely above labour, the daughters are hurried through the routine of boarding school instruction, and at an early period introduced into the gay world; and, thenceforth, their only object is amusement. Mark the different treatment, which the sons of these families receive. While their sisters are gliding through the mazes of the midnight dance, they employ the lamp, to treasure up for future use the riches of ancient wisdom; or to gather strength and expansion of mind, in exploring the wonderful paths of philosophy. When the youth of the two sexes has been spent so differently, is it strange, or is nature in fault, if more mature age has brought such a difference of character, that our sex have been considered by the other, as the pampered wayward babies of society, who must have some rattle put into our hands, to keep us from doing mischief to ourself or others?

Another difference in the treatment of the sexes is made in our country, which, though not equally pernicious to society, is more pathetically unjust to our sex. How often have we seen a student, who, returning from his literary pursuits, finds a sister, who was his equal in acquirements, while their advantages were equal, of whom he is now ashamed. While his youth was devoted to study, and he was furnished with the means, she, without any object of improvement, drudged at home, to assist in the support of the father's family, and perhaps to contribute to her brother's subsistence abroad; and now, a being of a lower order, the rustic innocent wonders and weeps at his neglect.

. . . .

Another errour is, that it has been made the first object in educating our sex, to prepare them to please the other. But reason and religion teach, that we too are primary existencies; that it is for us to move, in the orbit of our duty, around the Holy Centre of perfection, the companions, not the satellites of men; else, instead of shedding around us an influence, that may help to keep them in their proper course, we must accompany them in their wildest deviations.

I would not be understood to insinuate, that we are not, in particular situations, to yield obedience to the other sex. Submission and obedience belong to every being in the universe, except the great Master of the whole. Nor is it a degrading peculiarity to our sex, to be under human authority. Whenever one class of human beings, derive from another the benefits of support and protection, they must pay its equivalent, obedience.

. . . .

Neither would I be understood to mean, that our sex should not seek to make themselves agreeable to the other. The errour complained of, is that of the taste of men, whatever it might happen to be, has been made a standard for the formation of the female character. In whatever we do, it is of the utmost importance, that the rule, by which we work, be perfect. For if otherwise, what is it, but to err upon principle? A system of education, which leads one class of human beings to consider the approbation of another, as their highest object, teaches, that the rule of their conduct should be the will of beings, imperfect and erring like themselves, rather than the will of God, which is the only standard of perfection.

Having now considered female education, both in theory and practice, and seen, that in its present state, it is in fact a thing "without form and void," the mind is naturally led to inquire after a remedy for the evils it has been contemplating. Can individuals furnish this remedy? It has heretofore been left to them, and we have seen the consequence. If education is a business, which might naturally prosper, if left to individual exertion, why have legislatures intermeddled with it at all? if it is not, why do they make their daughters illegitimates, and bestow all their cares upon their sons?

It is the duty of a government, to do all in its power to promote the present and future prosperity of the nation, over which it is placed. This prosperity will depend on the character of its citizens. The characters of these will be formed by their mothers; and it is through the mothers, that the government can control the characters of its future citizens, to form them such as will ensure their country's prosperity. If this is the case, then it is the duty of our present legislators to begin now, to form the characters of the next generation, by controling that of the females who are to be their mothers, while it is yet with them a season of improvement.

But should the conclusion be almost admitted, that our sex too are the legitimate children of the legislature; and, that it is their duty to afford us a share of their paternal bounty; the phantom of a college-learned lady, would be ready to rise up, and destroy every good resolution, which the admission of this truth would naturally produce in our favor.

To shew that it is not a masculine education which is here recommended, and to afford a definite view of the manner in which a female institution might possess the respectability, permanency, and uniformity of operation of those appropriated to males; and yet differ from them, so as to be adapted to that difference of character and duties, to which the other sex should be formed, is the object of the following imperfect

Sketch of a Female Seminary

From considering the deficiencies in boarding schools, much may be learned, with regard to what would be needed, for the prosperity and usefulness of a public seminary for females.

I. There would be needed a building with commodious rooms for lodging and recitation, apartments for the reception of apparatus, and for the accommodation of the domestic department.

II. A library, containing books on the various subjects in which the pupils were to receive instruction; musical instruments, some good paintings, to form the taste and serve as models for the execution of those who were to be instructed in that art; maps, globes, and a small collection of philosophical apparatus.

III. A judicious board of trust, competent and desirous to promote its interests, would in a female, as in a male literary institution, be the corner stone of its prosperity. On this board it would depend to provide,

IV. Suitable instruction. This article may be subdivided under four heads.

1. Religious and Moral
2. Literary
3. Domestic
4. Ornamental

1. *Religious and Moral.* A regular attention to religious duties would, of course, be required of the pupils by the laws of the institution. The trustees would be careful to appoint no instructors, who would not teach religion and morality, both by their example, and by leading the minds of the pupils to perceive, that these constitute the true end of all education. . . .

2. *Literary Instruction.* To make an exact enumeration of the branches of literature, which might be taught, would be impossible, unless the time of the pupils' continuance at the seminary, and the requisites for entrance, were previously fixed. Such an enumeration would be tedious, nor do I conceive that it would be at all promotive of my object. The difficulty complained

of, is not, that we are at a loss what sciences we ought to learn, but that we have not proper advantages to learn any. Many writers have given us excellent advice with regard to what we should be taught, but no legislature has provided us the means of instruction. Not however, to pass lightly over this fundamental part of education, I will mention one or two of the less obvious branches of science, which, I conceive should engage the youthful attention of my sex.

It is highly important, that females should be conversant with those studies, which will lead them to understand the operations of the human mind. The chief use to which the philosophy of the mind can be applied, is to regulate education by its rules. The ductile mind of the child is intrusted to the mother: and she ought to have every possible assistance, in acquiring a knowledge of this noble material, on which it is her business to operate, that she may best understand how to mould it to its most excellent form.

Natural philosophy has not often been taught to our sex. Yet why should we be kept in ignorance of the great machinery of nature, and left to the vulgar notion, that nothing is curious but what deviates from her common course? If mothers were acquainted with this science, they would communicate very many of its principles to their children in early youth. . . . A knowledge of natural philosophy is calculated to heighten the moral taste, by bringing to view the majesty and beauty of order and design; and to enliven piety, by enabling the mind more clearly to perceive, throughout the manifold works of God, that wisdom, in which he hath made them all. . . .

3. *Domestic instruction* should be considered important in a female seminary. It is the duty of our sex to regulate the internal concerns of every family; and unless they be properly qualified to discharge this duty, whatever may be their literary or ornamental attainments, they cannot be expected to make either good wives, good mothers, or good mistresses of families: and if they are none of these, they must be bad members of society; for it is by promoting or destroying the comfort and prosperity of their own families, that females serve or injure the community. To superintend the domestic department, there should be a respectable lady, experienced in the best methods of housewifery, and acquainted with propriety of dress and manners. Under her tuition the pupils ought to be placed for a certain length of time every morning. A spirit of neatness and order should here be treated as a virtue, and the contrary, if excessive and incorrigible, be punished with expulsion. There might be a gradation of employment in

the domestic department, according to the length of time the pupils had remained at the institution. The older scholars might then assist the superintendent in instructing the younger, and the whole be so arranged, that each pupil might have advantages to become a good domestic manager by the time she has completed her studies.

This plan would afford a healthy exercise. It would prevent that estrangement from domestic duties, which would be likely to take place in a length of time devoted to study, with those, to whom they were previously familiar; and would accustom those to them, who, from ignorance, might otherwise put at hazard their own happiness, and the prosperity of their families.

These objects might doubtless be effected by a scheme of domestic instruction; and probably others of no inconsiderable importance. It is believed, that housewifery might be greatly improved, by being taught, not only in practice, but in theory. Why may it not be reduced to a system, as well as other arts? There are right ways of performing its various operations; and there are reasons why those ways are right; and why may not rules be formed, their reasons collected; and the whole be digested into a system to guide the learner's practice?

It is obvious, that theory alone, can never make a good artist; and it is equally obvious, that practice un-aided by theory, can never correct errors, but must establish them. . . .

In the present state of things, it is not to be expected, that any material improvements in housewifery should be made. There being no uniformity of method, prevail-ing among different housewives, of course, the communi-cations from one to another, are not much more likely to improve the art, than a communication, between two mechanics of different trades, would be, to improve each in his respective occupation. But should a system of prin-ciples be philosophically arranged, and taught, both in theory and by practice, to a large number of females, whose minds were expanded and strengthened by a course of literary instruction, those among them, of an investigating turn, would, when they commenced house-keepers, consider their domestic operations as a series of experiments, which either proved or refuted the system previously taught. They would then converse together like those, who practise a common art, and improve each other by their observations and experiments; and they would also be capable of improving the system, by de-tecting its errors, and by making additions of new prin-ciples and better modes of practice.

4. The Ornamental branches, which I should recom-

mend for a female seminary, are drawing and painting, elegant penmanship, music, and the grace of motion. Needle-work is not here mentioned. The best style of useful needle-work should either be taught in the domestic department, or made a qualification for entrance; and I consider that useful, which may contribute to the decoration of a lady's person, or the convenience and neatness of her family. But the use of the needle, for other purposes than these, as it affords little to assist in the formation of the character, I should regard as a waste of time.

The grace of motion, must be learnt chiefly from instruction in dancing. Other advantages besides that of a graceful carriage, might be derived from such instruction, if the lessons were judiciously timed. Exercise is needful to the health, and recreation to the cheerfulness and contentment of youth. Female youth could not be allowed to range unrestrained, to seek amusement for themselves. If it was entirely prohibited, they would be driven to seek it by stealth; which would lead them to many improprieties of conduct, and would have a pernicious effect upon their general character, by inducing a habit of treading forbidden paths. The alternative that remains is to provide them with proper recreation, which, after the confinement of the day, they might enjoy under the eye of their instructors. Dancing is exactly suited to this purpose, as also to that of exercise; for perhaps in no way, can so much healthy exercise be taken in so short a time. It has besides, this advantage over other amusements, that it affords nothing to excite the bad passions; but, on the contrary, its effects are, to soften the mind, to banish its animosities, and to open it to social impressions.

. . . .

It has been doubted, whether painting and music should be taught to young ladies, because much time is requisite to bring them to any considerable degree of perfection, and they are not immediately useful. Though these objections have weight, yet they are founded on too limited a view of the objects of education. They leave out the important consideration of forming the character. I should not consider it an essential point, that the music of a lady's piano should rival that of her master's; or that her drawing room should be decorated with her own paintings, rather than those of others; but it is the intrinsic advantage, which she might derive from the refinement of herself, that would induce me to recommend to her, an attention to these elegant pursuits. The harmony of sound, has a tendency to produce a correspondent harmony of soul; and that art, which obliges us to study nature, in order to imitate her, often enkindles the latent spark of taste—of sensibility for her beauties, till it glows to adoration for their author, and a refined love of all his works.

V. There would be needed, for a female, as well as for a male seminary, a system of laws and regulations, so arranged, that both the instructors and pupils would know their duty; and thus, the whole business, move with regularity and uniformity.

The laws of the institution would be chiefly directed, to regulate the pupil's qualifications for entrance, the kind and order of their studies, their behaviour while at the institution, the term allotted for the completion of their studies, the punishments to be inflicted on offenders, and the rewards or honours, to be bestowed on the virtuous and diligent.

The direct rewards or honors, used to stimulate the ambition of students in colleges, are first, the certificate or diploma, which each receives, who passes successfully through the term allotted to his collegiate studies; and secondly, the appointments to perform certain parts in public exhibitions, which are bestowed by the faculty, as rewards for superior scholarship. The first of these modes is admissible into a female seminary; the second is not; as public speaking forms no part of female education. The want of this mode, might, however, be supplied by examinations judiciously conducted. The leisure and inclination of both instructors and scholars, would combine to produce a thorough preparation for these; for neither would have any other public test of the success of their labors. Persons of both sexes would attend. The less entertaining parts, might be enlivened by interludes, where the pupils in painting and music, would display their several improvements. Such examinations, would stimulate the instructors to give their scholars more attention, by which the leading facts and principles of their studies, would be more clearly understood, and better remembered. The ambition excited among the pupils, would operate, without placing the instructors under the necessity of making distinctions among them, which are so apt to be considered as invidious; and which are, in our male seminaries, such fruitful sources of disaffection.

Perhaps the term allotted for the routine of study at the seminary, might be three years. The pupils, probably, would not be fitted to enter, till about the age of fourteen. Whether they attended to all, or any of the ornamental branches, should be left optional with the parents or guardians. Those who were to be instructed in them, should be entered for a longer term, but if this was a subject of previous calculation, no confusion would arise from it. The routine of the exercises being established by the laws of the institution, would be uniform, and publicly known; and those, who were previously acquainted with the branches first taught, might enter the higher classes; nor would those who entered the lowest, be obliged to remain during the three years. Thus the term of remaining at the institution, might be either one, two, three, four, or more years; and that, without interfering with the regularity and uniformity of its proceedings.

The writer has now given a sketch of her plan. She has by no means expressed all the ideas, which occurred to her concerning it. She wished to be as concise as possible, and yet afford conviction, that it is practicable, to organize a system of female education, which shall possess the permanency, uniformity of operation, and respectability of our male institutions; and yet differ from them, so as to be adapted, to that difference of character, and duties, to which early instruction should form the softer sex.

It now remains, to enquire more particularly, what would be the benefits resulting from such a system.

BENEFITS OF FEMALE SEMINARIES

In inquiring, concerning the benefits of the plan proposed, I shall proceed upon the supposition, that female seminaries will be patronized throughout our country.

Nor is this altogether a visionary supposition. If one seminary should be well organized, its advantages would be found so great, that others would soon be instituted; and, that sufficient patronage can be found to put one in operation, may be presumed from its reasonableness, and from the public opinion, with regard to the present mode of female education. It is from an intimate acquaintance, with those parts of our country, whose education is said to flourish most, that the writer has drawn her picture of the present state of female instruction; and she knows, that she is not alone, in perceiving or deploring its faults. Her sentiments are shared by many an enlightened parent of a daughter, who has received a boarding school education. Counting on the promise of her childhood, the father had anticipated her maturity, as combining what is excellent in mind, with what is elegant in manners. He spared no expense that education might realize to him, the image of his imagination. His daughter returned from boarding school, improved in fashionable airs, and expert in manufacturing fashionable toys; but, in her conversation, he sought in vain, for that refined and fertile mind, which he had fondly expected. Aware that his disappointment has its source in a defective education, he looks with anxiety on his other daughters, whose minds, like lovely buds, are beginning to open. Where shall he find a genial soil, in which he may place them to expand? Shall he provide them male instructors?—Then the graces of their per-

sons and manners, and whatever forms the distinguishing charm of the feminine character, they cannot be expected to acquire.—Shall he give them a private tutoress?
She will have been educated at the boarding school, and
his daughters will have the faults of its instruction
second-handed. Such is now the dilemma of many parents; and it is one, from which they cannot be extricated
by their individual exertions. May not then the only plan,
which promises to relieve them, expect their vigorous
support.

Let us now proceed to inquire, what benefits would
result from the establishment of female seminaries.

They would constitute a grade of public education,
superior to any yet known in the history of our sex; and
through them, the lower grades of female instruction
might be controlled. The influence of public seminaries,
over these, would operate in two ways; first, by requiring
certain qualifications for entrance; and secondly, by
furnishing instructresses, initiated in their modes of
teaching, and imbued with their maxims.

Female seminaries might be expected to have important and happy effects, on common schools in general;
and in the manner of operating on these, would probably place the business of teaching children, in hands
now nearly useless to society; and take it from those,
whose services the state wants in many other ways.

That nature designed for our sex the care of children, she has made manifest, by mental, as well as physical indications. She has given us, in a greater degree than men, the gentle arts of insinuation, to soften their minds, and fit them to receive impressions; a greater quickness of invention to vary modes of teaching to different dispositions; and more patience to make repeated efforts. There are many females of ability, to whom the business of instructing children is highly acceptable, and, who would devote all their faculties to their occupation. They would have no higher pecuniary object to engage their attention, and their reputation as instructors they would consider as important; whereas, whenever able and enterprizing men, engage in this business, they consider it, merely as a temporary employment, to further some other object, to the attainment of which, their best thoughts and calculations are all directed. If then women were properly fitted by instruction, they would be likely to teach children better than the other sex; they could afford to do it cheaper; and those men who would otherwise be engaged in this employment, might be at liberty to add to the wealth of the nation, by any of those thousand occupations, from which women are necessarily debarred.

But the females, who taught children, would have been themselves instructed either immediately or indirectly by the seminaries. Hence through these, the government might exercise an intimate, and most beneficial control over common schools. Any one, who has turned his attention to this subject, must be aware, that there is great room for improvement in these, both as to the modes of teaching, and the things taught; and what method could be devised so likely to effect this improvement, as to prepare by instruction, a class of individuals, whose interest, leisure, and natural talents, would combine to make them pursue it with ardour. Such a class of individuals would be raised up, by female seminaries. And therefore they would be likely to have highly important and happy effects on common schools.

It is believed, that such institutions, would tend to prolong, or perpetuate our excellent government.

An opinion too generally prevails, that our present form of government, though good, cannot be permanent. Other republics have failed, and the historian and philosopher have told us, that nations are like individuals; that, at their birth, they receive the seeds of their decline and dissolution. Here deceived by a false analogy, we receive an apt illustration of particular facts, for a general truth. The existence of nations, cannot, in strictness, be compared with the duration of animate life; for by the operation of physical causes, this, after a certain length of time, must cease; but the existence of nations, is prolonged by the succession of one generation to another, and there is no physical cause, to prevent this succession's going on, in a peaceable manner, under a good government, till the end of time. We must then look to other causes, than necessity, for the decline and fall of former republics. If we could discover these causes, and seasonably prevent their operation, then might our latest posterity enjoy the same happy government, with which we are blessed; or if but in part, then might the triumph of tyranny, be delayed, and a few more generations be free.

Permit me then to ask the enlightened politician of my country, whether amidst his researches for these causes, he cannot discover one, in the neglect, which free governments, in common with others, have shown, to whatever regarded the formation of the female character.

In those great republics, which have fallen of themselves, the loss of republican manners and virtues, has been the invariable precursor, of their loss of the republican form of government. But is it not in the power of our sex, to give society its tone, both as to manners and morals? And if such is the extent of female influence, is it wonderful, that republics have failed, when they calmly suffered that influence, to become enlisted in favour of luxuries and follies, wholly incompatible with the existence of freedom?

It may be said, that the depravation of morals and manners, can be traced to the introduction of wealth, as its cause. But wealth will be introduced; even the iron laws of Lycurgus could not prevent it. Let us then inquire, if means may not be devised, to prevent its bringing with it the destruction of public virtue. May not these means be found in education?—in implanting, in early youth, habits, that may counteract the temptations, to which, through the influence of wealth, mature age will be exposed? and in giving strength and expansion to the mind, that it may comprehend, and prize those principles, which teach the rigid performance of duty? Education, it may be said, has been tried as a preservative of national purity. But was it applied to every exposed part of the body politic? For if any part has been left within the pestilential atmosphere of wealth, without this preservative, then that part becoming corrupted, would communicate the contagion to the whole; and if so, then has the experiment, whether education may not preserve public virtue, never yet been fairly tried. Such a part has been left in all former experiments. Females have been exposed to the contagion of wealth without the preservative of a good education; and they constitute that part of the body politic, least endowed by nature to resist, most to communicate it. Nay, not merely have they been left without the defence of a good education, but their corruption has been accelerated by a bad one. The character of women of rank and wealth has been, and in the old governments of Europe now is, all that this statement would lead us to expect. Not content with doing nothing to promote their country's welfare, like pampered children, they revel in its prosperity, and scatter it to the winds, with a wanton profusion: and still worse,—they empoison its source, by diffusing a contempt for useful labour. To court pleasure their business,—within her temple, in defiance of the laws of God and man, they have erected the idol fashion; and upon her altar, they sacrifice, with shameless rites, whatever is sacred to virtue or religion.

.   .   .   .

But while, with an anguished heart, I thus depict the crimes of my sex, let not the other stand by and smile. Reason declares, that you are guiltier than we. You are our natural guardians,—our brothers,—our fathers, and our rulers. You know that our ductile minds, readily take the impressions of education. Why then have you neglected our education? Why have you looked with lethargic indifference, on circumstances ruinous to the formation of our characters, which you might have controlled?

But it may be said, the observations here made, cannot be applied to any class of females in our country.

True, they cannot yet; and if they could, it would be useless to make them; for when the females of any country have become thus debased, then, is that country so corrupted, that nothing, but the awful judgments of heaven, can arrest its career of vice. But it cannot be denied, that our manners are verging towards those described; and the change, though gradual, has not been slow: already do our daughters listen with surprise, when we tell them of the republican simplicity of our mothers. But our manners are not as yet so altered, but that, throughout our country, they are still marked with republican virtues.

The inquiry, to which these remarks have conducted us is this—What is offered by the plan of female education, here proposed, which may teach, or preserve, among females of wealthy families, that purity of manners, which is allowed, to be so essential to national prosperity, and so necessary to the existence of a republican government.

1. Females, by having their understandings cultivated, their reasoning powers developed and strengthened, may be expected to act more from the dictates of reason, and less from those of fashion and caprice.

2. With minds thus strengthened they would be taught systems of morality, enforced by the sanctions of religion; and they might be expected to acquire juster

and more enlarged views of their duty, and stronger and higher motives to its performance.

3. This plan of education, offers all that can be done to preserve female youth from a contempt of useful labour. The pupils would become accustomed to it, in conjunction with the high objects of literature, and the elegant pursuits of the fine arts; and it is to be hoped, that both from habit and association, they might in future life, regard it as respectable.

To this it may be added, that if housewifery could be raised to a regular art, and taught upon philosophical principles, it would become a higher and more interesting occupation; and ladies of fortune, like wealthy agriculturalists, might find, that to regulate their business, was an agreeable employment.

4. The pupils might be expected to acquire a taste for moral and intellectual pleasures, which would buoy them above a passion for show and parade, and which would make them seek to gratify the natural love of superiority, by endeavoring to excel others in intrinsic merit, rather than in the extrinsic frivolities of dress, furniture, and equipage.

5. By being enlightened in moral philosophy, and in that, which teaches the operations of the mind, females would be enabled to perceive the nature and extent, of that influence, which they possess over their children,

and the obligation, which this lays them under, to watch the formation of their characters with unceasing vigilance, to become their instructors, to devise plans for their improvement, to weed out the vices from their minds, and to implant and foster the virtues. . . .

Thus, laudable objects and employments, would be furnished for the great body of females, who are not kept by poverty from excesses. But among these, as among the other sex, will be found master spirits, who must have pre-eminence, at whatever price they acquire it. Domestic life cannot hold these, because they prefer to be infamous, rather than obscure. To leave such, without any virtuous road to eminence, is unsafe to community; for not unfrequently, are the secret springs of revolution, set in motion by their intrigues. Such aspiring minds, we will regulate by education, we will remove obstructions to the course of literature, which has heretofore been their only honorable way to distinction; and we offer them a new object worthy of their ambition; to govern, and improve the seminaries for their sex.

In calling on my patriotic countrymen, to effect so noble an object, the consideration of national glory, should not be overlooked. Ages have rolled away;— barbarians have trodden the weaker sex beneath their feet;—tyrants have robbed us of the present light of

heaven, and fain would take its future. Nations, calling themselves polite, have made us the fancied idols of
a ridiculous worship, and we have repaid them with
ruin for their folly. But where is that wise and heroic
country, which has considered, that our rights are
sacred, though we cannot defend them? that tho' a
weaker, we are an essential part of the body politic,
whose corruption or improvement must affect the
whole? and which, having thus considered, has sought
to give us by education, that rank in the scale of being,
to which our importance entitles us? History shows not
that country. It shows many, whose legislatures have
sought to improve their various vegetable productions,
and their breeds of useful brutes; but none, whose
public councils have made it an object of their deliber-
ations, to improve the character of their women. Yet
though history lifts not her finger to such an one, antici-
pation does. She points to a nation, which, having
thrown off the shackles of authority and precedent,
shrinks not from schemes of improvement, because
other nations have never attempted them; but which,
in its pride of independence, would rather lead than
follow, in the march of human improvement: a nation,
wise and magnanimous to plan, enterprising to under-
take, and rich in resources to execute. Does not every
American exult that this country is his own? And who

knows how great and good a race of men, may yet arise from the forming hand of mothers, enlightened by the bounty of that beloved country,—to defend her liberties, —to plan her future improvement,—and to raise her to unparalleled glory?

SELECTIONS FROM THE TEXTBOOKS OF
EMMA WILLARD

It has seemed wise to include in this source book selections from the prefaces of some of Mrs. Willard's best known textbooks because they reveal very clearly that the author had grasped, at least in part, certain modern principles of sound method in teaching. In her earliest work, the *Geography for Beginners* (1826) she criticizes the contemporary practice of training the memory at the expense of the other faculties, and depreciates the method of learning names of places, historic personages, and events without thought of their relationships. Furthermore she advocates teaching geography to beginners by *methods adapted to their age and understanding*. To this end she has reduced both the scope and amount of subject matter in her *Geography* to bring it within the capacity of young children to grasp. She declares herself "desirous that the child should understand as he goes rather than that he should go far." Adaptation of subject matter to the child's mind is further shown in Mrs. Willard's advocacy of a method of studying maps which was in sharp contrast to current practice and suggests that she was familiar with the revolutionary methods of the Swiss educational reformer Pestalozzi, who died the year after her little *Geography* was published. Briefly, Mrs. Willard suggests that the young child should begin his study of maps by drawing "a map of his own town"—Pestalozzi's method of "home geography." After he has begun to understand a map in relation to a locality, he can go on to study the map of the United States. Last, not first, as was customary, he may study the map of the world. Finally Mrs. Willard makes use of a conversational method in her little *Geography:* "Mother" and "Frank" carry on the conversation in each chapter—a method which she rightly believes more suitable to young pupils than the usual formal presentation of a subject.

The reader of Emma Willard's texts will be impressed by her emphasis on *methods of observation* or an appeal to the eye of the pupil by means of maps and charts. Like Pestalozzi she appears to have been in revolt against the purely verbal, memoriter educational methods of her age. Her theory of "observation by means of the senses" is shown not only in the *Geography for Beginners* but in her *Ancient Geography* (1833), her *Guide to the Temple of Time and Universal History for Schools* (1850), and her *Abridged History of the United States* or *Republic of America* (1852). In the *Ancient Geography* Mrs. Willard decries the method by which the child learns catalogues of names without learning *at the same time* their places on the map. She was led by experience to work out a plan for studying maps by means of a set of printed questions in an atlas which accompanied her *Ancient Geography*. Believing that maps of ancient times should faithfully reproduce the geography of *that time*, she sought to give pupils historically accurate maps to dispel their difficulty in distinguishing different periods of time on maps including centuries of history. A picture of the progress of the Roman Empire, illustrated by the course of the Amazon River appears as a frontispiece and shows her use of the senses to aid understanding. Another example of this method is seen in a quaint illustration of the *Temple of Time*, the great historic periods being represented as sections of the structure. In one of her later works—the *Abridged History of the*

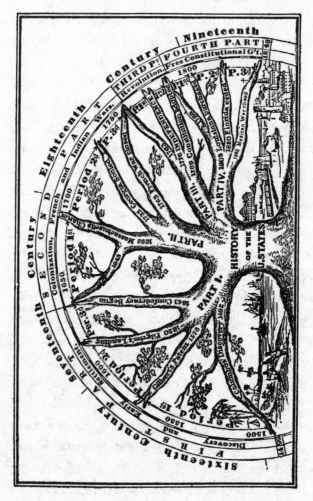

CHRONOGRAPHICAL PLAN

United States . . .—appears a curious "Chronograph-ical plan," illustrating the history of the United States, from the discovery of America to the middle of the nine-teenth century, by means of a giant tree with spreading branches. This illustration, which is reproduced, was but a small replica of a "large painted chronographer," which accompanied the text and was hung in full view of the class. By means of a pointer, skillfully used by the teacher, the pupil would learn to associate the great events of his country's history with their dates. If the plan were studied attentively the author believed it would "become a part of the mind of every attentive scholar."

The educator of the present may be disposed to ques-tion these devices in part; yet he cannot fail to perceive that they represent a marked advance over the dry and purely verbal schoolroom methods of Emma Willard's day.

GEOGRAPHY FOR BEGINNERS:

or the

INSTRUCTER'S ASSISTANT

in giving

FIRST LESSONS FROM MAPS

in the style of

FAMILIAR CONVERSATION

Accompanied with an Atlas

Being intended as the first, or introductory book, to a series of geographical works, by William C. Woodbridge, and Emma Willard; of which, the second book is entitled "The Rudiments of Geography," the third book, "Universal Geography."

By Emma Willard

Principal of Troy Female Seminary

Hartford:

Oliver D. Cooke & Co.

1826.

GEOGRAPHY FOR BEGINNERS

Preface

Maps may be said to be the written language of geography, and nothing can be taught until the pupils understand the medium through which they are to learn. The necessity of some work to assist instructers [*sic*] in teaching this language, became apparent to the authors of the system of which this is the first part, by the difficulties they had experienced themselves as teachers, and by the complaints of other instructers. The author of this little work, by adopting the conversation style, placed herself in a situation in which she could use illustrations which experience had taught her are intelligible to children; and her old pupils will recognize here the very same instructions which brought them to an understanding of the subject.

Authors have heretofore appeared to think that if they wrote a geography, they must make out an entire system. A book for children must be small, and hence they have stated more and more in generals, as they have gone downwards in the scale of age. This course appears to me the reverse of that which the structure of the mind requires. The author here only begins to teach the science. She has been desirous that the child should understand as he goes, rather than that he should go far. To accomplish the object of making the pupils understand the subject, the author has here entirely departed from the common arrangement. Instead of commencing the study of maps with the map of the world, which is much the most difficult for a child to understand, the pupil here begins, in the most simple manner imaginable, to draw the map of his own town. From this he goes to a map of the United States, merely containing the boundaries of the states, then to one on the common plan, and last in the course he takes the map of the world; omitting till this time the subject of latitude and longitude. The author having found the subject of latitude the most difficult part of her task, has devoted a considerable portion of her work to it; but no more than in her opinion is required by the difficulty and importance of this ground work of the whole science. She has left the subjects of religion, government, etc. entirely untouched. This work is large enough to begin with. A child of good abilities, with the opportunities of instruction afforded by a common school, will do well to learn it thoroughly in a year; and by this time his book will be worn out, and one of a new kind, like the second part of this system, will please him better.

It is not expected that the pupils who study this little book should be required to commit their lessons to memory; and hence, brevity of expression has not been studied. They are expected to answer such questions, as shall best draw out their comprehension of the subject, and as these questions ought to vary with the age and capacity of the pupil, as well as the length of time he has been studying, they must, in the opinion of the author, be left to the judgment of the teacher.

Although this method may not at first be quite so easy to teach as where pupils commit to memory, yet the ambitious instructer will find it for his ultimate interest to make his pupils understand, previously to the attempt to make them remember. He wishes to bring his pupils forward well prepared for their public examinations. If they learn merely by the order of the words, a single word misplaced may involve a mistake the most ridiculous. Whereas a pupil who understands the subject, will always be nearly, if not quite correct; or if he makes a mistake, it will be of the same kind as other people who understand a subject are liable to make.

The longer the author continues in the business of education, the more is she surprised at the narrowness of the former, and probably, of present exertions, when compared with the breadth of the field. Memory was almost the only faculty formerly cultivated. Much more attention is now paid than heretofore to the development of the reasoning powers. But there are many important faculties to which little attention is paid, and which might be improved by their proper exercise. The power of observation by means of the senses, and particularly that of sight, is of the greatest importance; and children should be put upon systematic courses of examining for themselves. An example of this may be here found in a plan of observation of the sun's apparent course. The faculty of calling up and keeping steadily before us absent objects of perception, and considering them under new arrangements, is also highly important; and an exercise perhaps better for this purpose than any other, because the objects can be more clearly conceived, is here prepared in the observation of the sun's apparent course in different latitudes.

Till the author sat down to the task of writing this elementary sketch, she had not supposed the capacity of children equal to understanding the appearance of the sun in the various latitudes. But on investigating the subject, she became satisfied that the bare statement of the phenomena, stripped of every hypothesis as to their causes, is not above the capacity of ordinary children of seven years old, and that it is precisely here that we should commence teaching them those fundamental truths of astronomy on which geography is founded. But the mind of the young pupil in this course of instruction should not be hurried. He should be permitted to dwell some time on one part of the subject, before he goes to another, till at length he can call up the image of the sun in all the various appearances of his daily course. That children can be made to understand thus far, is evident from considering that the simple conceptions, whose combinations form these pictures, are few, great, and well known to children. The several simple images which comprise the grand picture of the sun's appearance at the arctic circle—the broad, arched expanse of the visible heavens—their central point, the zenith, their boundary, the horizon, and, especially, that one grand object, which, during the day, there travels alone in his brightness—these images are as perfect in the mind of the child as in that of the poet or the astronomer; and, in fact, to teach him to dwell on them when they are not before him, and to form with them new combinations, may facilitate his becoming in future life either the one or the other.

Yet, in the culture of the mind, intellectual improvement should ever be held as secondary to moral. Would we teach to children candour, the first attribute of goodness, we must use it in our intercourse with them. Instead of endeavouring with pedagogical dignity, to impress them with a belief that we possess all knowledge, and that to us every thing is easy, the author or teacher should show them the difficulties of the subject, and let them know that where these exist, he and all others, men or children, must find the same. This the author has endeavoured to do, considering that such a course increases the efforts of the pupil by giving him correct and encouraging views of his own powers, while it tends to elevate and ennoble his character.

ANCIENT GEOGRAPHY
as connected with
CHRONOLOGY
AND PREPARATORY TO THE STUDY OF
ANCIENT HISTORY:
ACCOMPANIED WITH AN ATLAS

BY EMMA WILLARD

Author of "A Plan for Improving Female Education,
Addressed To The Legislature of New York," and
Principal of the Female Seminary at Troy

Compiled Chiefly from D'Anville, Adam, Lavoisne,
Malte-Brun, and Other Standard Works
To Which Are Added
PROBLEMS ON THE GLOBES
AND RULES FOR THE CONSTRUCTION
OF MAPS
To Accompany the Modern Geography By
WILLIAM C. WOODBRIDGE

Fifth Edition
Hartford:
Published by Oliver D. Cooke & Co.
1833.

ANCIENT GEOGRAPHY

Introduction

Although facts constitute a very important part of human knowledge, yet some persons find their recollection of past occurrences too indistinct and uncertain, to afford much light for the regulation of their conduct. Others, on the contrary, can rely on the correctness of their knowledge, and command the confidence of those whom they may wish to persuade. The superiority of the latter appears to me to result, in a great measure, from their having acquired a habit, not possessed by the former, of associating with events the time and the place in which they happened. If in teaching history, we can fix this habit in the mind of the pupil, while we give him a knowledge of its facts, we shall have accomplished two important objects at the same time.

To locate the events of history, requires a knowledge of ancient geography. This the pupil may obtain, either by examining maps as he proceeds with his history, or by studying them before he commences. But to require him to find on his map all the cities, mountains, &c. of which he reads, when he does not know in what country, or in what quarter of the globe they are situated, is to waste his time, and to discourage him in the outset from forming the habit which we wish. This he easily acquires when ancient geography is the introductory study. Not that we expect the mind of the scholar in either ancient or modern geography will contain at once the name of every place. He does not so much learn to do without his maps, as to use them with ease and pleasure.

The habit of locating facts once acquired, improvement in geography and in the history of past or passing events, will go on and mutually aid each other. The event will be remembered from the place, and the place from the event. By a knowledge of geography the reasoning powers are enabled to assist the memory, both in receiving and retaining historical events. The pupil will be able of himself to fill up a sketch, whether imperfect from a defect in original information or subsequent forgetfulness. . . .

The systems of Ancient Geography which I examined, were not adapted to my peculiar views. I therefore arranged one for the use of my pupils, the same which forms the basis of that which is here offered to the public. The works which I examined, contained catalogues of names, that the pupil is expected to learn from the book; or which he will learn in this way if permitted, rather than to be at the trouble of searching them out upon the maps. The consequence of this will be, that he will associate them with that page of his book from which he learned them, rather than those places on the map to which they belong. Were learners never to see the names of places till they see them on their maps, the association of the name with the place would be more perfect. With this view, I wished the pupils of my school to have nothing more to aid them in studying their maps than a set of questions, which would lead them to form this association, and which would also assist their teacher, by enabling the class definitely to understand what they were required to learn; these questions should, however, be accompanied by explanations of those parts of the maps, which would otherwise be obscure.

With respect to the succession of events, without particular care to prevent it, the study of ancient geography will tend to confuse instead of enlightening the learner. Descriptions of places, as they were in different ages of the world, are almost unavoidably set in books, without any other distinction of time, than the general terms ancient and modern; while all ancient empires and cities, whether coexistent or not, are placed together on the maps. But the terms ancient and modern, as applied to geography, can no more be contrasted than a point and a line; the one referring to the present merely, the other, to that long course of ages, during which those numerous important changes in society took place, which it is the business of history to describe. Maps, of historical or progressive geography, are pictures of things in a changing state; and such, to be accurate, can take in but a single point of time.[1] Considering these circumstances, it became a problem with me, to find some method of introducing my pupils to the study of history, by which they might habitually acquire clear ideas of the dates of events, while they were learning their places; and to solve this has been a leading object of that part of the work which they are required to study after the questions on the maps.

Although of the three ideas, an event, its place, and date, the event is most important, yet it is the visible representation of the place, with which, for the purpose of permanent impression, we should seek to associate the event and its date. Hence the importance of requiring the student to examine his maps frequently, while he is studying historical facts. In chronological charts,

[1] For a further illustration of those principles, see article on Difficulties occurring in the study of Ancient Maps, &c.

events are connected with the time in which they happened by means of visible objects, as colours, &c., but the associations are arbitrary; whereas, in the method here proposed, the visible object with which the fact is connected, is the true geographical representation of the place in which it happened.

．　　．　　．　　．　　　．　　．　　．　　．

Persons who have in their youth read history without method will feel with the author, that they have lost much by not being taught some such plan, as is laid down in the directions for making maps. In reviewing the long line of time which has elapsed since the date of history, it would be absurd to expect that in each point which composes it, we should have clear ideas of every remarkable contemporaneous event. At the same time, every person possessed of historical knowledge, must be sensible that there are in his mind certain points of time, from which, like eminences in a road, he can look abroad and discover the remarkable objects there existing together; and that, were it otherwise, his knowledge would run into one confused mass. In this plan, we erect these eminences for the pupil, that thus they may be made at proper intervals, and that by contemplating them in early youth, the impressions may be permanent. We plant him, as it were, upon one of these spots of time; we detain him upon it until he has collected every important fact, and we oblige him to delineate it in a manner sensible to the eye, and giving him ever after a command of the whole at a single glance.

GUIDE TO THE TEMPLE OF TIME AND UNIVERSAL HISTORY FOR SCHOOLS

PREFACE

In offering to the public this book, with its companion, the *Temple of Time,* the author cannot bring her mind to frame an apology; because she is soberly impressed with a belief, that she is rendering a service to the cause of educational science. The object of aiding the young teacher, as well as of assisting the pupil, has brought into it, much of the experience of thirty years devoted to instructing, as well as of long and matured reflection, on the special subject of educational history.

And in no way does the author conceive that she could better serve her country, than in awakening a taste for history, and putting its grand outline more within the power of universal acquisition, in every common school, throughout our wide republic. This, if it stands, must remain by avoiding the rocks, upon which all former republics have foundered. History must make them known; and not merely to here and there a solitary statesman. *"We the people"* must have an enlightened will; or power with us, may, like a steam-engine on a wrong track, carry destruction in its course. And if the people are to understand history, then it must be taught in the people's schools.

The method of pointer-teaching is here circumstantially explained; not only according to long experience and the examination of different schools in our own country, but with an attention to what has, in this respect, been done abroad. This method has, besides the eminent advantage of impression by the eye, an immense multiplying power over that great article *Time, which is all that is given by our Creator wherein to do the work of improvement;* so that it may be propounded as an axiom in teaching, that, *that teacher is the best, who best employs his own time, and that of his pupils.* Suppose a teacher has sixty scholars. Three minutes' separate teaching to each makes up the master's three hours: whereas, if, with an unexpensive apparatus, such as we offer him, he teaches his whole school together fifteen minutes, then this multiplied by sixty, (the number of pupils who enjoy the master's instruction,) multiplies his fifteen minutes, to fifteen hours.

We have great need to quicken the process of education, to meet the demands of a new age of steam and electricity. We must learn to value the time of children.

Among other things, the teacher must seek for the means, by which, like Providence, he can make one exercise answer many good purposes. For learning to read, each scholar in a class must practise by himself. Why not in the advanced class put a multiplied value on the reading hour, by considering the importance of what may be acquired,—and also the superior manner of reading to be obtained, where the subject is regarded as the main thing, and the *manner* left in a degree to regulate itself? Wherever manner alone is regarded, it degenerates into mannerism. . . . Suppose you have a class of ten, and you require for to-morrow's lesson that each pupil shall read for the information of the whole class, who are to be afterwards questioned by the teacher, one of the short biographies contained in this little book,—and you give each his choice to select and study well his part. Then you have given him an interest in looking over the biographies to select;—you permit him to study his own part, and you bring down the public opinion of his class to bear upon the distinctness and propriety of his enunciation, for they must understand him. And what is the object of ever reading aloud, but solely to benefit others?

These remarks refer not to the reading of history only, but they apply to other important subjects of study, which are also suitable for reading aloud. But history is eminently a suitable subject.—It deals in narrative.—It is truth,—nothing is genuine history which is not; and if duly set forth, it shows the right and the wrong of human actions,—for the instruction of individuals and of nations.

ABRIDGED HISTORY

of the

UNITED STATES

or,

REPUBLIC OF AMERICA

New and Enlarged Edition

BY EMMA WILLARD

New York

Published by A. S. Barnes & Co.

Cincinnati:—H. W. Derby & Co.

1852.

ABRIDGED HISTORY OF THE UNITED STATES

Introduction

1. The large painted chronographer, prepared, to accompany this work, is to be hung in full view of the class, and the teacher furnished with a pointing rod about four feet in length, black at the end, as the paper of the chronographer is white.[1]

2. *The proper use of the pointer constitutes an intelligible language addressed to the eye.* Therefore, the person using it should use it significantly, and never otherwise, and should always point in the same manner when he means the same thing.

. . . .

4. Whenever the teacher is using the pointer, to teach the chronographer, the pupil must give his eye, his ear, and his mind; and then the chronographer will, by a mysterious process of mind, be formed within, and become a part of the mind of every attentive scholar— where he may, ever after, have the plan, and read the principal dates of his country's chronology. But in order

[1] *Cf.* p. 86.

to have the internal chronographer perfect, it is necessary to observe attentively, and to learn patiently, at various times and in repeated lessons, the different parts of the one presented to the eye.

PART II

CATHERINE BEECHER

Life of Catherine Beecher.

Suggestions Respecting Improvements in Education.

Essay on The Education of Female Teachers for the United States.

An Address on Female Suffrage Delivered in the Music Hall of Boston in December, 1870.

Letters to the People on Health and Happiness.

Calisthenics.

CATHERINE BEECHER

(Facing page 114)

CATHERINE BEECHER, PIONEER OF EDUCATION IN THE WEST

In the first year of the nineteenth century, a century pregnant with growth and change in the life of young America, Catherine Beecher was born in the little town of Easthampton, Long Island. The daughter of the Rev. Lyman Beecher, D.D., eminent pastor of the Congregational Church and member of a distinguished family of preachers and writers, this girl baby was destined to become one of the ablest advocates of an extended and improved education for women of her generation. Born on September 6, 1800, she was the oldest daughter in a family of thirteen children, which included the brilliant pulpit orator Henry Ward Beecher and the gifted writer Harriet Beecher Stowe.

Fortunately for her biographers, Catherine Beecher published in 1874 her *Educational Reminiscences and Suggestions* from which the most significant facts of her life may be drawn. She tells the reader that it was her "good fortune to be born in humble circumstances" and to be called upon early in life to assist her mother, and later her stepmother, in caring for the younger children and in performing household tasks. It was no doubt in this difficult school of experience that Catherine Beecher acquired that valuable knowledge of home management and child care which in later years she put at the service of the public in her books on domestic economy.

The Rev. Lyman Beecher was, according to his daughter, an imaginative, impulsive man, passionately fond of children, whom he delighted to nurse and tend. Although he "excelled in argumentation" and was a preacher of distinction he appears to have been somewhat averse to hard study. Catherine's mother, on the other hand, was a kind but undemonstrative parent, calm, self-possessed, and with a marked practical and executive ability. She appears to have had real talent as a mathematician, solving problems "because she enjoyed that kind of mental effort," and revealing a native gift in logical reasoning that led her husband to remark that she was the only person he had met whom he felt to be "fully his equal in an argument." These contrasting characteristics in her parents—the warm, imaginative, nurturing impulses of the father and the practical, self-controlled, intellectual qualities of the mother —led Miss Beecher shrewdly to observe that "there is in mind no distinction of sex, and . . . much that passes for natural talent is mainly the result of culture." [1]

The early education of little Catherine was undertaken by her mother and her mother's sisters. She was taught to read, write, and spell, and was even given a peep into the mysteries of geography and arithmetic. The girl's mother taught her to draw and paint in water colors —"accomplishments" that were highly esteemed for girls in those days. Apparently Catherine was a merry, happy little girl with a wholesome zest for play and little interest in the household duties which she was compelled to perform before she could join her playfellows out of doors. But her mother firmly held her to the performance of her domestic tasks and trained her "to perfect and uncomplaining obedience." In her *Reminiscences* Miss Beecher pays tribute to her mother's kindly discipline and ascribes her accomplishments in later

[1] *Educational Reminiscences and Suggestions,* p. 14, J. B. Ford and Co., New York, 1874.

years to the early training which modified her natural "defects" of carelessness and love of play. After "years of drilling," she tells us, "I learned to perform whatever I attempted; at least with moderate excellence."

In 1810 Dr. Beecher accepted a call to Litchfield, a lovely old town in the Connecticut hills. Here was an academy kept by Miss Sarah Pierce—a school destined later to become famous—to which Catherine was sent at the age of ten. Apparently little was taught the "young ladies" of the academy in those days beyond the three R's, drawing, painting, and music. Young Catherine, having little zest for learning at this time, became very adroit in guessing the answers to questions addressed to her and by "a few snatches at books" managed to slip through her school tasks with little difficulty. So skillful did she become in evading serious study, that she relates in her *Reminscences* that one of her teachers complimented her as "the busiest of all creatures in doing nothing."

But this happy, relatively care-free life came to an end when Catherine was sixteen with the death of her mother. Soon her aunt Esther came to manage her brother's household and Catherine found numerous responsibilities, hitherto unknown, laid upon her young shoulders. Two years later her father married again, this time a widow with several young children of her own. Once more, Miss Beecher relates, she was trained by her stepmother in those habits of order, system, and neatness which were foreign to her nature.

When she was almost twenty, the need for self-support led Miss Beecher to prepare herself to teach, the only vocation open to young women at that time. She began taking lessons on the piano, and although blessed with no marked talent for music, she was fortunate in having a very thorough and painstaking teacher. Spurred by the earnest desire to make herself independent, Miss Beecher attained such proficiency that, at the end of a year and a half, she was recommended to teach in a girls' school in New London and to play in an Episcopal church. In addition she taught drawing and painting, arts which she studied for a short time under the direction of a well-trained teacher. But, as she justly comments, "at that period very humble performances in these accomplishments gave satisfaction."

At the age of twenty-two Miss Beecher commenced her preparation to teach the so-called "higher branches" by spending the winter with a friend of the family who gave her what she describes as "most thorough instruction." Then it was that she was introduced to the mysteries of Daboll's Arithmetic, much in vogue. Then, also, it was that she acquired a serious interest in the underlying principles of arithmetic—in contradistinction to a half-comprehending practice—which led her subsequently to publish an arithmetic of her own. In her *Reminiscences* she tells the reader that Professor Olmstead of Yale wrote her in friendly fashion about this her first publication:

"Your Arithmetic I have put into the hands of my children, giving it a decided preference over those in common use. Reflecting how I might best serve you, it has occurred to me that when your revised edition is out, I may write a notice of it, more or less extended, for the *Christian Spectator,* which could be used by your publisher."

Despite her success in teaching arithmetic, Miss Beecher testifies that of all the studies she ever pursued it was the most difficult and uninteresting. She attributes her success to the fact that the practical usefulness of the subject stimulated an indirect interest in mastering it.

During this winter of study she "went through Day's Algebra, a few exercises in Geometry, a work on Logic, and two small works prepared for schools, on Chemistry and Natural Philosophy."

Thus equipped for teaching she opened a school for girls in Hartford, Connecticut, with the assistance of a younger sister. The work began in the upper chamber of a store with an attendance of seven girls—none under twelve years. In a short time her school became so well patronized that it was moved into the basement of a church where nearly a hundred girls were assembled. It is easy to picture the difficulties which Miss Beecher encountered in conducting a school with no financial backing and almost no equipment. The seminary boasted only one room, no large map or globes, most of the time no blackboard, and only two teachers. In these days of generous school equipment, the task that faced Miss Beecher and her sister seems almost hopeless. Yet she attacked it cheerfully, using the practical domestic training she had received in finding "the best way of doing anything and everything" to the greatest advantage. Owing to the faulty primary education of her pupils, she was forced to organize different grades of classes in all the elementary branches as well as in the higher studies. In consequence barely ten minutes could be allotted to each class for recitation; and even then the harried head mistress was forced to employ her brightest pupils as assistant teachers. Later she reduced this method to a system which proved of the utmost value. In her *Reminiscences* Miss Beecher writes feelingly of her struggle to teach her "young ladies" under the conditions just described:

It could not "be ascertained how much was clearly understood, or how much was mere memorizing of words. To preserve order while attending to recitations all in one room, to hear such a succession of classes in so many different studies, to endure such a round of confusion, haste, and imperfection, with the sad conviction that nothing was done as it should be, now returns to memory as a painful and distracting dream. The only pleasant recollection is that of my own careful and exact training under my most accurate and faithful brother, Edward, and my reproduction of it to my sister, Harriet, and two others of my brightest pupils. With them, I read most of Virgil's Æneid and Bucolics, a few of

Cicero's orations, and some of the finest parts of Ovid—portions of the last being turned into English verse by one of the class." [1]

When Miss Beecher was twenty-three years old a tragic event caused her the deepest sorrow of her life. The ship *Albion,* on which was embarked her fiancé, Professor Fisher of Yale, was lost in a storm off the Irish coast. The shock to Miss Beecher was devastating. Her brother, Henry Ward Beecher, once said that under the strain of grief and disappointment she all but lost her religious faith. For a long time her only consolation was found in absorbing work.

After four years of laborious effort Miss Beecher became convinced, as was Mrs. Willard before her, that no educational institutions could rest upon a firm basis or furnish sound and thorough instruction to its students unless it could command adequate financial support. Therefore she drew up the plan of the Hartford Seminary, submitted it to the leading citizens of Hartford and asked that the building be erected by public subscription. Her own account of the mental disturb-

[1] *Reminiscences,* pp. 31–32 (ed. 1874).

ance which her unheard-of request stirred in these worthy gentlemen deserves to be given in full:

"Many of them were surprised and almost dismayed at the 'visionary and impracticable' suggestion, and when it became current that I wanted a study hall to hold one hundred and fifty pupils, a lecture room, and six recitation rooms, the absurdity of it was apparent to most of the city fathers, and, with some, excited ridicule. But the more intelligent and influential women came to my aid, and soon all I sought was granted. This was my first experience of the moral power and good judgment of American women, which has been my chief reliance ever since." [1]

Under the vastly improved conditions of the new seminary, Miss Beecher was able to carry out some of her long-cherished plans. She divided her girls into small classes, approximately equal in acquirements and ability, and put them in charge of teachers who were expected to teach only two or three branches. With each teacher she associated the most able pupils in her class as assistants, thus giving these students some preparation to become teachers. She herself trained her

[1] *Op. cit.*, p. 33.

teachers in methods of instruction and the teachers passed on these methods to their pupil assistants. In all this reorganization Miss Beecher was seeking to realize the ideal of years—a division of work and responsibility within the school similar to that of a college.

After six years of apparently successful management of her seminary, Miss Beecher was convinced that her school could never approach the standards and organization of the American college without endowments. What she desired was a faculty of coequal teachers, sharing the heavy responsibility of school administration and deciding on new policies by majority vote. Furthermore she longed for adequate library facilities and apparatus for teaching. She believed that by restricting the amount of instruction required of the teachers, each one could secure time for self-improvement and for the advancement of her own department or departments. Needless to say no such conditions existed in the Hartford Seminary. No library or apparatus was provided nor could they possibly be secured from tuition fees. Miss Beecher's dissatisfaction with this situation was intensified by a heavy load of work. She was compelled to add to her duties as instructor the further tasks of training her teachers and assuming all the cares of school management and finances. Not having the vigorous constitution of an Emma Willard, it is not surprising that she suffered a nervous breakdown under the strain and was obliged to withdraw from the school. The seminary was continued after her departure but sustained a decline for many years.

In 1833 Dr. Lyman Beecher received a call to a pastorate in the city of Cincinnati and Miss Beecher accompanied her family to the new home. For months she was obliged to lead a quiet, restful life until her health was restored. However, her fame had preceded her and she was almost immediately solicited to establish a much needed higher school for girls in Cincinnati. At last she consented to secure trained teachers for the proposed school and do all her health would permit to carry it on. She herself asked for and received five hundred dollars for furniture and apparatus, and later she secured four of her former teachers and pupils in the Hartford Seminary to staff the new school, which was called the Western Female Institute.

Organized on the college plan of coequal teachers, so ardently advocated by Miss Beecher, the school had soon enrolled more students than it could accommodate. Under Miss Beecher's leadership, a fine building was then rented in a central yet retired location surrounded by trees. As the building was for sale, Miss Beecher was influential in organizing a committee of citizens to raise funds to purchase it. But she tells us "there was no man to take the lead, and the committee were absorbed in their own affairs"—a comment on the vitality of the interest in higher education for girls in the thirties.

In this school Miss Beecher developed still further the calisthenic exercises she had originated in her Hartford school. These exercises were accompanied by music and were designed "to secure all of the advantages supposed to be gained in dancing schools" together with graceful bodily movements to the sound of music. The interest in a "lady-like" form of physical training was only just feebly stirring in America at this time, under the influence of Dio Lewis and of Catherine Beecher herself, whose writings on calisthenics, as well as the exercises she originated, were extensively used both in the East and the West. An excellent conception of what physical training for women meant a century ago can be gained from Miss Beecher's *Reminiscences:*

"When physical education takes the proper place in our schools, young girls will be trained in the classrooms to move head, hands, and arms gracefully; to sit, to stand, and to walk properly, and to pursue calisthenic exercises for physical development as a regular school duty as much as their studies. And these exercises, set to music, will be sought as the most agreeable of school duties." [1]

During the five years when Miss Beecher was directly interested in the Western Female Institute, she began to write those books on domestic economy which form one of her most important contributions to the education of women. One was a manual of useful information for housewives on a wide variety of subjects concerned with home management; the other was a textbook for use in girls' schools. The latter work was introduced into various schools in both the East and West. Unquestionably the writer's advocacy of do-

[1] *Op. cit.,* pp. 85–86.

mestic science as a study and her admirable books in this field had considerable influence in forming a public opinion favorable to the inclusion of this subject in the curriculum of the new public schools.

At this period of her life Catherine Beecher, like Emma Willard, became profoundly interested in the problem of securing a better training for the women teachers who were flocking into education as the only field of skilled work open to them. For nearly forty years Miss Beecher labored by traveling, lecturing, and writing to organize societies for training teachers and especially to work out plans for supplying trained teachers to staff the new schools everywhere springing up in the frontier states and territories. In an address read at the annual meeting of the National Lyceum in 1835 she "plead the causes of the two million children of our country without teachers, and of the multitudes of educated Christian women vainly seeking for schools." From that time Miss Beecher dedicated herself heart and soul to the work of securing educated and trained women in the East who would be willing to act as "missionary teachers" in the newly settled and ignorant sections of the West and the South.

Her first step in carrying out this large project was to consult women of influence in both the East and West. After securing their approval of her plans, she then organized a committee of women in Cincinnati who were willing to work for the realization of the plan. At the same time her brother-in-law Professor Calvin Stowe, the husband of her sister Harriet, organized a committee of gentlemen from several of the religious denominations of Cincinnati to coöperate with the women. Not content with these efforts Miss Beecher wrote the book entitled *American Women, Will You Save Your Country?* which was published anonymously by Harper's and widely circulated. This ringing challenge, together with a circular from the Cincinnati committees, was sent to numerous influential women of the chief Protestant sects in the East and West. Soon contributions for the cause began to pour in to Miss Beecher. Even more encouraging was the news that the "Boston Ladies' Society for Promoting Education at the West" had been organized and had actively thrown itself into the work. For several years this society devoted its energies with much success to sending "excellent teachers" (in Miss Beecher's words) to the western schools.

In carrying on this nation-wide campaign it is interesting to note Miss Beecher's tactics. Her first efforts were always spent in enlisting the interest and active aid of leading women. Indeed she tells us:

"From the commencement of my educational efforts, it was my practice always to seek the counsel of intelligent housekeepers, mothers and school-teachers, and I have never adopted any important plans or measures till I had secured the approval of women of high culture who had gained practical wisdom in performing such duties." [1]

Another bit of strategy employed by Miss Beecher was to obtain, if possible, the coöperation of religious denominations in her plans for extending education. In an age when organized religion played a far more important rôle in all large social undertakings than at present, this was undoubtedly sound tactics. Moreover, Miss Beecher showed her understanding of the popular mind by securing her brother Thomas, or if possible,

[1] *Reminiscences,* p. 101.

some other interested gentleman to deliver her addresses for her. Well did she know the public scorn and disapproval that were showered at that time upon those "strong-minded females" who dared to address an audience from a public platform; and she did not propose to injure the cause to which she was so earnestly committed by overstepping the narrow bounds of "female propriety" in the forties.

As her educational plans expanded and a wider interest in them was quickened, it became evident to Miss Beecher that an agent would have to be appointed who could devote his entire time to promoting the work. This would entail the raising of a salary sufficiently adequate to attract a man of education, public spirit, and organizing ability. To this end Miss Beecher made a tour of many of the larger cities accompanied by her brother Thomas. Meetings of women were organized at which her brother delivered the address she had prepared appealing for financial aid. In the end she received pledges and assurances of help sufficient to insure the payment of a suitable salary; and later with the aid of her father and of Professor Stowe, she was able to enlist the services of ex-Governor Slade of Vermont as educational agent.

While the new agent undertook in the West the work of lecturing and organizing committees to aid in finding schools in need of teachers and caring for the teachers sent from the East, Miss Beecher remained in the East to select the teachers willing to take the long, uncomfortable journey to the western frontiers to teach in raw, young communities where schools were being established. In course of time a difference of viewpoint and policy developed in the work of ex-Governor Slade and Miss Beecher. The former severed his connection with Calvin Stowe's Cincinnati committee and organized at Cleveland the Board of National Popular Education. Unfortunately the constitution of the board made no provision for an agent specially intrusted with the task of aiding the eastern teachers to find schools and homes; nor did it provide funds to assist them in emergencies of illness and unemployment. In consequence the evils which Miss Beecher had foreseen came to pass. The board not only did not find enough places for the two groups of

133

teachers Miss Beecher sent out, but not a few of these young women found themselves in serious difficulties and wrote appealing letters to Miss Beecher to help them out—which she attempted to do. Another obstacle to the realization of her scheme was the fact that the young teachers from the East, finding themselves eagerly courted as wives in settlements where women were a precious minority, often married and left the field of their missionary labors. Therefore it may be said that, although Miss Beecher's project of providing an adequate supply of trained teachers for the frontier schools of the West accomplished considerable good, yet it could hardly be said to have been a complete or permanent success. Perhaps the most valuable result of the movement was the education of public opinion to the need for common schools and trained teachers which was inaugurated by Miss Beecher.

It was not long before Miss Beecher, with character-istic energy, was launching a new educational plan which had for years been a cherished dream. This was the establishment of higher schools for women on the college model at central points in the West, organized with a faculty of coequal teachers instead of with a principal and subordinates. Her plan provided for boards of trustees and staffs of teachers, representing the chief religious denominations and "thus avoiding the great obstacles of sectarianism." It further provided for a normal department in each school "including every advantage obtained in Eastern Normal Schools"; for a boarding house "so endowed as to serve as a home for teachers in all emergencies"; for committees of women in both the East and West to select and train teachers from both the state and "abroad"; and for the employment of "women as agents, with proper salaries, as men employ agents of their own sex, to raise up and endow their colleges and professional schools." [1]

In behalf of her scheme Miss Beecher visited Indianapolis, Davenport, Quincy, Milwaukee, and other cities consulting with their leading citizens concerning the plan. An active interest in the proposed institution was aroused in the young city of Milwaukee, then boasting a population of twenty thousand inhabitants, many of them new settlers from Germany and Scandinavia. Unfortunately the citizens were too poor to carry out in full Miss Beecher's plan, although she contributed

[1] *Reminiscences*, p. 138.

funds of her own and donations from women in the East. Despite the generous efforts of citizens, it was found impossible to raise the necessary amount to purchase land or erect a suitable building. Yet a school partly realizing the plan was established in Milwaukee on a precarious economic foundation, the library and apparatus were furnished, and soon one hundred young women were enrolled as students. Filled with ardent concern for the success of this struggling institution, Miss Beecher toured the East with a clerical associate and raised among her friends and well-wishers sufficient funds to purchase a site for the projected building.

Realizing to the full the necessity of having continuous aid and financial support behind the new school, Miss Beecher organized in New York City two meetings of women of large experience and public spirit who were selected from eight different denominations to avoid sectarian difficulties. To their number were added several business and professional men of high character and influential social position. Out of these two meetings, held on May 8th and 15th, 1852, grew a permanent and useful organization incorporated as the

American Woman's Education Association. Immediately funds were raised and a building erected in Milwaukee according to the plan drawn by Miss Beecher. The object of the association as set forth in its constitution was: "To aid in securing to American women a liberal education, honorable position, and remunerative employment *in their appropriate profession,* by means of *endowed* institutions, on the college plan of organization; these schools to include all that is gained by normal schools, and also to train women to be healthful, intelligent and successful wives, mothers and housekeepers." For years the association met annually in New York to receive reports from its agents in the field and to prepare its own reports of plans and progress, which are valuable sources of information to the student of the education of women.

A word should be said regarding certain emphatic phrases in the constitution of the association, which definitely reflect Miss Beecher's firm convictions. The stress laid on *endowed* institutions is of course due to the settled belief of the founder of the association—shared with Emma Willard—that no schools for women could prosper unless they were assured of steady financial support. The emphasis laid on woman's "appropriate profession" sheds light on Miss Beecher's deeply rooted philosophy concerning the sphere and duties of her sex. Like Emma Willard, she had scant sympathy with the infant movement to secure larger legal and political rights for women. In her crystallized judgment there were but three spheres of work legitimately open to women—the domestic and the fields of nursing and education. Over and over again in her writings she has reiterated her belief that if educated women would but fit themselves to be intelligent mothers, nurses, domestic helpers, and teachers, there would be no women workers left in factories and no feminine discontent expressing itself in suffrage movements. It would no doubt be highly illuminating to this educational pioneer if her spirit could revisit the twentieth-century world and view an economic situation in which probably nine million women, married and unmarried, are engaged in well-nigh all the gainful employments listed in the United States Census. What would be the effects on national economy, and domestic economy as well, if these millions of women were restricted to the tasks of household workers, nurses, and teachers?

As a result of the active efforts of the American Woman's Education Association another school, similar to that in Milwaukee, was established at Dubuque, Iowa. In these institutions were educated from two to three hundred young women. Both schools had Normal departments and sent out well-educated and trained teachers of which the West had urgent need. To Miss Beecher's disappointment the departments of health and domestic economy were not endowed and organized in these schools, probably owing to lack of funds. Certainly the plans she drew up for these departments were not only ambitious but remarkably sensible and far-sighted, in view of modern developments. For example she proposed that the principal of the health department should "maintain a system of physical training in which both teachers and pupils would take part, . . . to enforce all the laws of health; to lecture on the distinctive duties of wife and mother to the graduating classes; to teach the classes in physiology; . . . and, finally, to supervise the whole establishment as it [sic] respects warming and ventilation."

Likewise the plan provided that the principals of the domestic department "would have the charge of all relating to the æsthetic, social, and domestic, and teach both the science and practice of Domestic Economy. . . . The supervision of the school and family building would belong to this department. Each of these departments would be provided with modern dwelling houses, illustrating proper and tasteful modes of construction, furniture, ornamentation, warming and ventilation." [1]

It was further planned that the family in each house should consist of the principal, associate principal, and ten of the pupils of the school who would do all the family work except the heavy labor. By a system of rotation each student would be trained in "every occupation included in family life." It is hardly necessary to point out that many departments of domestic economy in modern high schools and colleges have not yet realized this excellent plan.

In her later years, Miss Beecher devoted herself more exclusively to writing, publishing, one after another, new editions of those works on domestic economy and calisthenics for which she is famous. Her earlier books entitled *Evils Suffered by American Women and Ameri-*

[1] *Reminiscences,* pp. 157–158.

can Children (1846) and *True Remedy for the Wrongs of Women* (1851) were ringing appeals to her sex to abandon mills and factories and fit themselves for their true vocations as housekeepers, nurses, and teachers, leaving the realms of business, finance, the professions, and government wholly to men, "designed by God" to be preëminent in these fields. A large part of the sums received in royalties on these books Miss Beecher devoted to helping on the cause of women's education to which she was so loyally committed.

In her declining years Miss Beecher made her home in Elmira, New York, home of the first college for women in the North. Always a woman of weak physique, she carried on her constructive and often exhausting educational work under great physical handicaps. In her old age she suffered much from lameness and nervous debility. Yet she preserved her native cheerfulness and sense of humor and beguiled the time by singing and playing on the piano and guitar in the old-fashioned manner of her youth. On May 12, 1878, she slipped out of life at the age of seventy-eight, ripe in years and in accomplishments.

It has been said of Miss Beecher that "she had a mind

full of original vigor, but without much imagination; it was perhaps the want of this that made some of her schemes impracticable." This may be true. Certainly her largely conceived ambitions were not fully realized. Yet it may well be asked what advocate of great social improvements has ever lived to see the full fruitage of his labors. Catherine Beecher's reach exceeded her grasp, as is true of all really significant apostles of a new and better order.

SUGGESTIONS

RESPECTING

IMPROVEMENTS IN EDUCATION

PRESENTED TO THE TRUSTEES

of the

HARTFORD FEMALE SEMINARY

and published at their request

BY CATHERINE E. BEECHER

———

Hartford:

PACKARD & BUTLER

Hudson and Skinner, Printers

MDCCCXXIX

SUGGESTIONS RESPECTING IMPROVEMENTS IN EDUCATION

The following selection is taken from one of the earliest of Miss Beecher's writings. At this time (1829) she was head of the Hartford Female Seminary, an incorporated school, for which a building had been erected through the contributions of citizens of Hartford. In the treatise Miss Beecher pleads with great earnestness that teaching be made an honorable profession instead of "the resource of poverty." She here first states the conviction, which remained with her throughout life, that the true professions of women are those of mother and teacher; that these arduous duties are of the utmost importance to society and require that women be thoroughly prepared by education to carry them on. The author further urges such "division of labour" in girls' schools as is found in men's colleges in order that teachers may properly prepare themselves to teach a few subjects rather than make a superficial effort to teach a dozen. She refers to the "sickness of heart" which attacked her in former years at the close of the school day because she well knew that her attempts to instruct pupils in eight to twelve branches were time wasted, since "nothing was done well." In her closing appeal she urges women to abandon the "useless inactivity" into which they too often sink after their school days are over and realize their "delightful duty" to cultivate and develop immortal minds.

———————

Most of the defects which are continually discovered and lamented in present systems of education may be traced, either directly or indirectly to the fact, that the *formation* of *the minds of children has not been made a profession securing wealth, influence, or honour,* to those who enter it.

The three professions of law, divinity, and medicine, present a reasonable prospect of reputation, influence and emolument to active and cultivated minds. The mercantile, manufacturing and mechanical professions present a hope of gaining at least that *wealth* which can so readily purchase estimation and influence. But the profession of a *teacher* has not offered any such stimulus.

It has been looked upon as the resource of poverty, or as a drudgery suited only to inferior minds and far beneath the aims of the intellectual aspirant for fame and influence, or of the active competitor for wealth and distinction. The consequence of this has been, as a general fact, that this profession has never, until very recently, commanded, or secured the effort of *gifted minds*. . . .

It is to *mothers,* and to *teachers,* that the world is to look for the character which is to be enstamped on each succeeding generation, for it is to them that the great business of education is almost exclusively committed. And will it not appear by examination that neither mothers nor teachers have ever been properly educated for their profession. What is *the profession* of a *Woman?* Is it not to form immortal minds, and to watch, to nurse, and to rear the bodily system, so fearfully and wonderfully made, and upon the order and regulation of which, the health and well-being of the mind so greatly depends?

But let most of our sex upon whom these arduous duties devolve, be asked; have you ever devoted any time and study, in the course of your education, to any preparation for these duties? Have you been taught any thing of the structure, the nature, and the laws of the body, which you inhabit? Were you ever taught to understand the operation of diet, air, exercise and modes of dress upon the human frame? Have the causes which are continually operating to prevent good health, and the modes by which it might be perfected and preserved ever been made the subject of any *instruction*? Perhaps almost every voice would respond, no; we have attended to almost every thing more than to this; we have been taught more concerning the structure of the earth; the laws of the heavenly bodies; the habits and formation of plants; the philosophy of languages; more of *almost any thing,* than the structure of the human frame and the laws of health and reason. But is it not the business, the *profession* of a woman to guard the health and form the physical habits of the young? And is not the cradle of infancy and the chamber of sickness sacred to woman alone? And ought she not to know at least some of the *general principles* of that perfect and wonderful piece of mechanism committed to her preservation and care?

The *restoration* of health is the physician's profession, but the *preservation* of it falls to other hands, and it is believed that the time will come, when woman will be taught to understand something respecting the construction of the human frame; the physiological results which will naturally follow from restricted exercise, unhealthy modes of dress, improper diet, and many other causes, which are continually operating to destroy the health and life of the young.

Again let our sex be asked respecting the instruction they have received in the course of their education, on that still more arduous and difficult department of their profession, which relates to the *intellect* and the *moral susceptibilities*. Have you been taught the powers and faculties of the human mind, and the laws by which it is regulated? Have you studied how to direct its several faculties; how to restore those that are overgrown, and strengthen and mature those that are deficient? Have you been taught the best modes of *communicating* knowledge as well as of *acquiring* it? Have you learned the best mode of correcting bad *moral* habits and forming good ones? Have you made it an object to find how a selfish disposition may be made generous; how a reserved temper may be made open and frank; how pettishness and ill humor may be changed to cheerfulness and kindness? Has any woman studied her profession in this respect? It is feared the same answer must be returned, if not from all, at least from most of our sex. No; we have acquired wisdom from the observation and experience of others, on almost *all other* subjects, but the philosophy of the direction and control of the human mind has not been an object of thought or study. And thus it appears that tho' it is woman's *ex-*

press business to rear the body, and form the mind, there is scarcely anything to which her attention has been less directed. . . .

If all females were not only well educated themselves, but were prepared to communicate in an easy manner their stores of knowledge to others; if they not only knew how to regulate their own minds, tempers and habits, but how to effect improvements in those around them, the face of society would speedily be changed. The time *may* come when the world will look back with wonder to behold how much time and effort have been given to the mere cultivation of the memory, and how little mankind have been aware of what every teacher, parent, and friend could accomplish in forming the social, intellectual and moral character of those by whom they are surrounded. . . .

Another fundamental difficulty in education, has resulted from the fact that the great principle of the *Division* of *Labour,* which ensures improvement and success in all the several arts and sciences has never until very recently, and only in a few instances, been introduced into *school education.*

In our *colleges,* where our elder youth are assembled, those whose minds have, to some degree, been made discriminating by discipline, and mature by age, this principle to a considerable extent, has been introduced, so that ordinarily, not more than one or two branches are committed to the care of one person. But in schools for females, and for childhood, where the mind is very immature, the powers of attention weak, the habits of discrimination and investigation unformed, no such division of labour has been thought necessary. One teacher has been considered sufficient to teach Reading, Spelling, Grammar, Geography, Arithmetic, Composition, History, Natural Philosophy, Chemistry, and the list in many cases might be extended to some eighteen or twenty different branches. Beside this, pupils have been admitted promiscuously at every age and at every stage of advancement, so that often several classes must be formed *in each branch*. In addition to all, *one room* has been considered sufficient for every recitation, and every school exercise, as well as for the place devoted to study. As for apparatus for explanation and illustration, it has been entirely out of the question; and had it been furnished, it would have been of little avail to teachers debarred from their duty and privilege of *communicating* knowledge, and condemned to spend their *whole time* in endeavouring to discover *how much pupils have learned from books,* without the aid of a teacher.

This Institution was established to make the experiment of the benefits of the division of labour in a female school of the higher order, and though the experiment has been but a short and imperfect one, it is believed that it may be presented as an example in proof that *a division of labour* is the true principle both of *success* and of *economy* in education. But the beneficial operation of this principle as tested in this Institution, cannot be fairly appreciated, except by a comparison with the results of former modes of instruction.

There are obvious reasons why it would be both invidious and indecorous to compare this, with other schools which have not adopted the same general plan. The only comparison which can be made is with the present and former mode of conducting this school, and a statement of the different results, so far as the writer can determine them. In attempting this the writer asks indulgence for speaking so freely of what may perhaps be called *her own affairs*. It certainly would be much more agreeable, could *facts* be stated without any allusion to any personal concern, that the writer may have had in effecting them.

This school was commenced in the spring of the year 1823 by two associate teachers. At that time it was a general feeling in the community that the excellence of a school depended in a great degree upon the *number* of *branches* in which the teacher professed to instruct, and also in some measure upon the *difficulty* and *uncommonness* of these branches; so that most of the popular advertisements of the day, purported that one person proposed to teach in from *ten* to *twenty* different pursuits, and these including often times various languages, and many of the studies pursued in our colleges. In compliance with custom, the teachers of this school proposed thus to teach in the various departments of literature and science.

The school increased for two or three years, till gradually the number had risen from fifteen to nearly one hundred; thus indicating that the *public* at least, considered it as good as ordinary schools of that character. Being accommodated with only one room, not more than two teachers could be employed at the same time, and it generally was the case that from eight to twelve branches were taught every day, beside the exercises in writing, reading, spelling and upon the slate. In several of these branches, owing to difference in age and capacities, one, two, or three classes were necessarily instituted, making the number of recitations so great that not more than eight, ten, or at most fifteen minutes could be allowed, even to the most difficult and important recitations. . . .

By the time the duties of the day were over, the care of governing, the vexations of irregularities and mischief, the labour of hearing such a number and variety of lessons, and the *sickness of heart* occasioned by feeling that *nothing was done well,* were sufficient to exhaust the animal strength and spirits, and nothing more could be attempted, till the next day arose to witness the same round of duties. While attempting to teach in this manner, the writer felt that no single duty of a teacher could possibly be performed. The pupils could not be taught to *read* or *write* or *spell,* though many of them came most imperfectly prepared even in these very first parts of education. No study could be understood by the pupil, nor in a single branch could the teacher prepare *herself* to instruct. All was a round of haste, imperfection, irregularity, and the mere mechanical commitment of words to memory, without any chance of obtaining a clear and definite idea of a single branch of knowledge.

The review of those days is like the memory of a painful and distracting dream, and nothing but the hope of remedy and relief, when time should have gained a measure of public approbation and confidence, sustained and encouraged, while continuing the most unremitting efforts to accomplish all that *could* be done in such unfavorable circumstances. During the fourth year a communication was made to some of the leading citizens of Hartford, stating many of the evils which are the consequences of the present modes of conducting schools, and proposing a plan for a remedy. The result was the endowment and incorporation of the Hartford Female Seminary, the erection of the present convenient accommodations, and a partial supply of some of the most necessary facilities for instruction.

The following will exhibit some general outline of the method adopted, and of the success which has been the result.

The accommodations consist of one large hall, where the pupils assemble for all the general exercises of the school, and where they are expected to study when not engaged in other school duties. Besides this, there are *ten* other rooms employed for the other purposes of instruction, such as a Library, Lecture Room and Recitation Rooms. Most of these are furnished with black boards, and in some cases all the sides of the rooms are devoted to this purpose. *Eight teachers* are employed, and to each one, the care of not more than one or two branches is committed. Besides these, there is a class of *eight* or *ten assistant pupils* employed, who are preparing to become teachers, and who have the care of instructing one class an hour each day, in some particular branch. Each teacher receives her classes at regular hours, in a recitation room devoted exclusively to her use, and is allowed an *hour* for the purpose of hearing and explaining each lesson. Each teacher is considered as responsible for the improvement of all who attend to the study in which she instructs. It is expected that by reading and study, she will qualify herself to teach it *thoroughly* and at the close of the term, that she conduct the public examination of her classes in this particular branch.

Beside the division of labour in the communication of knowledge, one other arrangement has greatly contributed to the best interests of the school. One teacher is exclusively occupied, as *governess,* in enforcing the rules of neatness, order, and propriety, and in administering the government of the school. She sits in the Hall which is devoted to study, to see that perfect quiet is preserved; she is the person from whom all permissions are sought; she attends to the regular departure and return of the classes to and from the recitation rooms; and in short relieves the other teachers from all care except that of communicating knowledge. No arrangement has more effectually contributed to the comfort and prosperity of the institution than this.

In *classing* the school, one great object has been to have the classes *small,* and to place in the same class only those who are equal in intellect, scholarship, and advancement in each study. By this arrangement no pupil is detained by companions who cannot equal her in progress, nor hurried forward to accommodate others, and obliged to pass over her lessons in a superficial manner. And thus when a pupil is found capable and willing to advance faster than her companions, she can be removed to another class and be placed among her equals. It has usually been found that in such studies as Arithmetic, Geometry and Algebra, from *six* to *ten* pupils are as many as one teacher can profitably instruct in a class, while in such studies as Geography and Grammar, the numbers in the classes vary from twelve to eighteen or twenty.

In giving instruction efforts have been made to use *objects of sight,* as much as possible, in every school exercise. Most operations in Arithmetic, Geometry and Algebra, are performed with chalks on the black boards around the sides of the room. The lessons in Geography are accompanied by the exercise of drawing a map of the country recited, upon the black board, by every pupil. The maps are accurately constructed, by the aid of tables and graduated measures. In teaching Grammar, Latin, Mental Philosophy, and almost every branch, the black board presents its visible signs to aid in recalling ideas. In Chemistry, Natural Philosophy, and other branches where apparatus is ordinarily used, this principle is of course adopted.

Another object aimed at is, not only to communicate ideas to the pupils, but to prepare them to *communicate them properly to others*. It is with this object in view, that the pupils are particularly required in the branch of Arithmetic (which is considered the most difficult and abstruse) to enter into a minute analysis and explanation of every process, in order that they may not only understand it themselves, but be prepared to communicate it to others. In various other school exercises, the pupils are instructed to make this a definite object of attention, as what is eminently fitted to promote their future usefulness. . . .

It has not been from mere theory, but as the result of observation and experience, that the opinion has been adopted, that however great may be the difference of capacities in *different individuals,* yet the faculties of the *same mind,* may by proper culture be all nearly equally developed. An ordinary mind, cannot, by any process, be made a superior one; but where we see indications of any extraordinary talent, every *other* faculty may by proper culture be brought to nearly equal perfection, *provided* the task be undertaken, before the mind is too far developed and advanced. There is no dispute on the point that some minds naturally have a strong *bias* for certain pursuits; that under the influence of this prepossession, these favorite objects occupy the mind, and thus strengthen and develop the particular faculties, which are thus kept in constant exercise; but this does not decide that if extra stimulus were applied to exercise and improve the *other* faculties, they might not advance in nearly equal proportion. The only difficulty to be apprehended is, that the natural bias may prove more powerful than any applied stimulus.

But the common and almost universal method adopted, both by parents and teachers, when any particular taste or bias has been the means of rendering some particular faculty of mind predominant and distinguished, has been, to bestow all the care of cultivation in developing it more fully, while other powers of mind which no particular predilection calls into exercise, are left to inactivity and neglect. Thus the mind becomes irregular and distorted, and all that is gained in one particular is lost in others, perhaps of superior importance.

If it be claimed that it is necessary to the *improvement of the several arts and sciences,* that *man* should turn his attention exclusively to some one particular department, and thus prevent the equilibrium or character desired, it may be granted to *one* sex, but it is not necessary for *woman.* On the contrary, a *well balanced mind* is the greatest and best preparative for her varied and complicated duties. Woman, in her sphere of usefulness, has an almost equal need of all the several faculties. She needs the discrimination, the solidity, and the force of character which the cultivation of the reasoning powers confers; she needs the refinement of taste, the chastened glow of imagination, the powers of quick preception, and of ready invention. Which of these shall we say a woman may dispense with in preparing herself for future duties.

May we not ascribe to this defect in education, the not unreasonable prejudice which has existed against *learned ladies?* Those who have been ambitious to maintain that character, by following the bias of a literary taste, too often have cultivated certain powers of mind in a disproportionate extent, and destroyed that true balance of mind which is so necessary for a woman, in forming a just estimate of her relative duties, as well as for the faithful discharge of them. . . .

It may be said, and said truly, that women are not prepared by *sufficient knowledge* to become teachers in many branches. But they *can be prepared,* and where they are not so well qualified as one of the other sex, they so often excel in patience and persevering interest, as to more than counter-balance the deficiency.

The writer cannot but believe, that all female institutions, for these and *many other reasons* ought to be conducted exclusively by females, *so soon as suitable teachers of their own sex can be prepared*. And is it not an indication that such is the will of Providence, when we see a *profession,* offering influence, respectability and independance, thrown open to woman? Until this day no other profession could with propriety admit the female aspirant, nor till this day has the profession of a teacher been the road to honour, influence, and emolument. But the feelings of enlightened society are fast changing on this momentous subject. Men of learning, genius, and enterprize are entering this long neglected profession, bringing the aid of their honours, influence, and talents to render it both lucrative and respectable. The time is not far distant when it will become an honourable profession, and beneath its liberal portal, woman is gladly welcomed to lawful and unsullied honours. Here, all that stimulus of motive which animates the other sex in their several professions, may be applied to quicken and animate her energies. *She* also, can discern before her the road to honourable independance, and extensive usefulness, where she need not outstep the prescribed boundaries of feminine modesty, nor diminish one of those retiring graces that must ever constitute her most attractive charms.

Woman has been but little aware of the high incitements that should stimulate to the cultivation of her noblest powers. The world is no longer to be governed by *physical* force, but by *the influence which mind exerts over mind*. How are the great springs of action in the political world put in motion? Often by the secret workings of a *single mind,* that in retirement plans its schemes, and comes forth to execute them only by presenting motives of prejudice, passion, self-interest or pride to operate on other minds. . . .

It is believed that the time is coming, when educated females will not be satisfied with the present objects of their low ambition. When a woman now leaves the immediate business of her own education how often, how generally do we find her sinking down into almost useless inactivity. To enjoy the social circle, to accomplish a little sewing, a little reading, a little domestic duty, to while away her hours in self-indulgence, or to enjoy the pleasures of domestic life, these are the highest objects at which many a woman of elevated mind and accomplished education aims. And what does she find of sufficient interest or importance to call forth her cultivated energies and warm affections?

But when the cultivation and development of the immortal mind shall be presented to woman as her especial and delightful duty, and that too, *whatever be her relations in life;* when by example, and by experience she shall have learned her power over the intellect and the affections; when the enthusiasm that wakens energy and interest in all other professions shall animate in this; then we shall not find woman returning from the precincts of learning and wisdom, merely to pass lightly away the bright hours of her maturing youth. We shall not so often find her seeking the light device to embroider on muslin and lace, but we shall see her, with the delighted glow of benevolence, seeking for *immortal minds,* whereon she may fasten durable and holy impressions, that shall never be effaced or wear away. Where does the painter or the poet turn, without finding in the glowing beauties of nature materials to employ their wonder-working powers; and where can woman turn, without discovering the gems of intellect, and buds of immortality, that she may gather and train for the skies?

AN ESSAY

on the

EDUCATION OF FEMALE TEACHERS

written at the

REQUEST OF THE AMERICAN LYCEUM

and

Communicated at their annual meeting,—
New York, May 8th, 1835.

═══════

BY CATHERINE E. BEECHER

═══════

Published at the desire of a meeting of Ladies
in New York.

NEW YORK:

Van Nostrand & Dwight, 146 Nassau St.
Cincinnati—Corey & Fairbanks.

1835

ESSAY ON THE EDUCATION OF FEMALE TEACHERS

Catherine Beecher's *Essay on the Education of Female Teachers* reveals a remarkable grasp of the deplorable condition of popular education in the new republic of America, in a period prior to the adoption by states of the policy of taxation for the support of public schools. Miss Beecher is one of the earliest group of writers who saw at the same time the national need of educated teachers and the possibility of meeting that need by drawing upon a large supply of unmarried women who desired employment. Her cautious and tentative suggestion with regard to giving "titles of honor" to well-educated women, her recognition that such a procedure would "provoke needless ridicule and painful notoriety" furnish clear evidence of the popular attitude toward "learned females." The conservative character of all Miss Beecher's theories of women's education—relatively liberal though they were when viewed from the standpoint of her age—is seen in her strong insistence on fitting women for a purely domestic sphere with the sole exception of the vocation of teaching.

The topic proposed for consideration in this essay cannot properly be presented, without previously adverting to certain difficulties in regard to female education; and, in the same connection, suggesting the most practicable methods of securing their remedy.

One of the first objects that need to be attempted in regard to female education, is to secure some method of rendering female institutions permanent in their existence, and efficient in perpetuating a regular and systematic course of education. This is secured for the other sex, by institutions so endowed that the death or removal of an individual does not hazard their existence or character. They continue year after year, and sometimes for ages, maintaining the same system of laws, government, and course of study. But in regard to female institutions, every thing is ephemeral; because, in most cases, every thing depends upon the character and enterprise of a single individual. A school may be at the height of prosperity one week, and the next week entirely extinct. Communities seem almost entirely dependent upon chance, both for the character and the perpetuity of schools. If good teachers stray into their bounds, they are fortunate; if poor ones, they have no remedy. Thus the character, the conduct, and the continuance of those who are so extensively to mould the character of the future wives and mothers of this nation, are almost entirely removed from the control of those most deeply interested.

One method which tends to remedy this evil is, the investment of property in buildings, furniture, and apparatus devoted to this object, under the care of a suitable corporate body. It thus becomes the business of certain responsible men, that the property thus invested shall secure the object for which it has been bestowed. But this method alone will not avail, for though the probabilities are greater that endowed institutions will be well sustained, it is often found that they do fail in securing a systematic and perpetuated plan of education. There needs to be added a well devised plan of government and course of study, together with that division of labor existing in colleges, which secures several able instructors to the same institution, and in such a way that the removal of any one teacher does not interrupt the regular system of the institution.

That this can be accomplished in regard to female seminaries, as well as those for the other sex, is no longer problematical, for it has already been done; and what has been, can be done again. One female institution, at least, can be referred to, in which a regular system of government and instruction has been carried on for a course of years, until an adequate number of teachers and pupils has been fitted to perpetuate the system, so that as one teacher after another was called away, others were prepared to take their places; and thus the whole number of teachers, from the principal to the lowest monitor, has been repeatedly changed, and yet the same system and course of study have been preserved; while there is as fair a prospect of future perpetuity as is afforded by most of our colleges.

Another object to be aimed at in regard to female education is, a remedy for the desultory, irregular, and very superficial course of education now so common in all parts of our country. When young men are sent to obtain a good education, there is some standard for judging of their attainments; there are some data for determining what has been accomplished. But, in regard to females, they are sent first to one school, and then to another; they attend a short time to one set of studies, and then to another; while everything is desultory, unsystematic, and superficial. Their course of study is varied to suit the notions of parents, or the whims of children, or the convenience of teachers; and if a young lady secures a regular and thorough course of education, it is owing either to the uncommonly good sense and efforts of parents, or to the rare occurrence of finding teachers sufficiently stationary and persevering to effect it.

The remedy for this evil (in addition to what is suggested in previous remarks) is to be sought in cooperating efforts among the leading female schools in the country, to establish a uniform course of education, adapted to the character and circumstances of females, to correspond with what is done in colleges for young gentlemen. The propriety of giving titles of honor to distinguished females who complete such a course, may well be questioned. It certainly is in very bad taste, and would provoke needless ridicule and painful notoriety. But if leading female institutions combine to establish a regular course of study, which is appropriate and complete, it will prove an honor and advantage to young ladies to have it known that their education is thus secured; and it will also prove an advantage to the schools that thus gain the reputation of sending out uniformly well educated pupils. Other schools will gradually adopt the same plan; and thus the evils alluded to will, to a great extent, be remedied. These measures will have the same effect on female education, as medical and theological schools have upon those professions. They tend to elevate and purify, although they cannot succeed in banishing all stupidity and empiricism.

Another object to be aimed at in regard to female education is, to introduce into schools such a course of intellectual and moral discipline, and such attention to mental and personal habits, as shall have a decided influence in fitting a woman for her peculiar duties. What is the most important and peculiar duty of the female sex? It is the physical, intellectual, and moral education of children. It is the care of the health, and the formation of the character, of the future citizen of this great nation.

Woman, whatever are her relations in life, is necessarily the guardian of the nursery, the companion of childhood, and the constant model of imitation. It is her hand that first stamps impressions on the immortal spirit, that must remain forever. And what demands such discretion, such energy, such patience, such tenderness, love, and wisdom, such perspicacity to discern, such versatility to modify, such efficiency to execute, such firmness to persevere, as the government and education of all the various characters and the tempers that meet in the nursery and school-room? Woman also is the presiding genius who must regulate all those thousand minutiae of domestic business, that demand habits of industry, order, neatness, punctuality, and constant care. And it is for such varied duties that woman is to be trained. For this her warm sympathies, her lively imagination, her ready invention, her quick perceptions, all need to be cherished and improved; while at the same time those more foreign habits, of patient attention, calm judgment, steady efficiency, and habitual self-control, must be induced and sustained.

Is a weak, undisciplined, unregulated mind, fitted to encounter the responsibility, weariness, and watching of the nursery; to bear the incessant care and perplexity of governing young children; to accommodate with kindness and patience to the peculiarities and frailties of a husband; to control the indolence, waywardness, and neglect of servants; and to regulate all the variety of domestic cares? The superficial accomplishments of former periods were of little avail to fit a woman for such arduous duties; and for this reason it is, that as society has been advanced in all other improvements, the course of female education has been gradually changing, and some portion of that mental discipline, once exclusively reserved for the other sex, is beginning to exert its invigorating influence upon the female character. At the same time the taste of the age is altered; and, instead of the fainting, weeping, vapid, pretty play-thing, once the model of female loveliness, those qualities of the head and heart that best qualify a woman for her duties, are demanded and admired.

None will deny the importance of having females properly fitted for their peculiar duties; and yet few are aware how much influence a teacher may exert in accomplishing this object. School is generally considered as a place where children are sent, not to form their habits, opinions, and character, but simply to learn from books. And yet, whatever may be the opinion of teachers and parents, children do, to a very great extent, form their character under influences bearing upon them at school. . . .

Nor is the course of study and mental discipline of inferior consequence. The mere committing to memory of the facts contained in books, is but a small portion of education. Certain portions of time should be devoted to fitting a woman for her practical duties: such, for example, as needlework. Other pursuits are designed for the cultivation of certain mental faculties, such as *attention, perseverance,* and *accuracy.* This for example, is the influence of the study of the mathematics; while the conversation and efforts of a teacher, directed to this end, may induce habits of investigation and correct reasoning, not to be secured by any other method. Other pursuits are designed to cultivate the taste and imagination: such as rhetoric, poetry, and other branches of polite literature. Some studies are fitted to form correct moral principles, and strengthen religious obligation: such as mental and moral philosophy, the study of the evidences of Christianity, the study of the Bible, and of collateral subjects. Other studies are designed to store the mind with useful knowledge: such, for example, as geography, history, and the natural sciences. The proper selection and due proportion of these various pursuits, will have a decided influence in forming the mental habits and general character of the pupils.

Another important object in regard to female education is, the provision of suitable facilities for instruction, such as are deemed indispensable for the other sex, particularly apparatus and libraries.

While the branches now included in a course of education for females of the higher circles have increased, till nearly as much is attempted, as, were it properly taught, is demanded of young men at college, little has been done to secure a corresponding change, in regard to the necessary facilities to aid in instruction.

To teach young men properly in chemistry, natural philosophy, and other branches of science, it is deemed necessary to furnish a teacher for each separate branch, who must be prepared by a long previous course of study, who shall devote his exclusive attention to it, and who shall be furnished with apparatus at the expense of thousands of dollars; while, to aid both teachers and pupils, extensive libraries must be provided, and all at public expense.

But when the same branches are to be taught to females, one teacher is considered enough to teach a dozen such sciences, and that too without any apparatus, without any qualifying process, and without any library.

If females are to have the same branches included in their education as the other sex, ought there not to be a corresponding change to provide the means for having them properly taught; or are our sex to be complimented with the intimation that a single teacher, without preparatory education, without apparatus, and without libraries, can teach young ladies what it requires half a dozen teachers, fitted by a long course of study and furnished with every facility of books and apparatus, to teach young gentlemen? We certainly are not ambitious of such compliments to the intellectual superiority of our sex. It is true such extensive public endowments are not needed for females as for the other sex, because their progress in many of the sciences never needs to be so extensive: but, if these branches are to constitute a part of female education, is not *something* of this kind demanded from public munificence, that all be not left to the private purse of the teacher, who must furnish it from slender earnings, or remain unsupplied?

But the most important deficiency, and one which is equally felt by both sexes, is the want of a system of moral and religious education at school, which shall have a *decided influence* in forming the character, and regulating the principles and conduct, of future life. . . .

In regard to education, the world is now making experiments, such as were never made before. Man is demanding disenthralment, alike from physical force, and intellectual slavery; and, by a slow and secret process, one nation after another is advancing in a sure, though silent progress. Man is bursting the chains of slavery, and the bonds of intellectual subserviency; and is learning to think, and reason, and act for himself. And the great crisis is hastening on, when it shall be decided whether disenthralled intellect and liberty shall voluntarily submit to the laws of virtue and of Heaven, or run wild to insubordination, anarchy, and crime. The great questions pending before the world, are simply these: are liberty and intelligence, without the restraints of a moral and religious education, a blessing, or a curse? Without moral and religious restraints, is it best for man to receive the gift of liberty and intelligence, or to remain coerced by physical force, and the restraints of opinions and customs not his own?

The master-spirits of the age are watching the developments as they rise, and making their records for the instruction of mankind.

And what results are already gained? In England, the experiment has been made by the sceptical Brougham; and, at great expense, knowledge has gone forth with increasing liberty, and all who have witnessed the results are coming to the conviction, that increase of knowledge, without moral and religious influence, is only increase of vice and discontent. And what are the results of the experiment in France? The statistics of education show, that the best educated departments are the most vicious, and the most ignorant are the freest from crime. And, in that country, where the national representatives once declared that Christianity should be banished, and the Bible burnt, and the Sabbath annihilated, we now find its most distinguished statesmen and citizens uniting in the public declaration, that moral and religious education must be the foundation of national instruction. Victor Cousin, one of the most distinguished philosophers of the age, and appointed by the King of France to examine the various systems of education in Europe, has reported, as the result of his investigations, that education is a blessing, just in proportion as it is founded on moral and religious principles.

Look, again, at Prussia! with its liberal and patriotic monarch, with a system of education unequalled in the records of time, requiring by law that all the children in the nation be sent to school, from the first day they are seven years of age, till the last day they are fourteen, with a regular course of literary and scientific instruction, instituted for every school, and every teacher required to spend three years in preparing for such duties; while, on an average, one teacher is furnished for every ten pupils through the nation. The effects of merely intellectual culture soon convinced the monarch and his counsellors that moral and religious instruction must be the basis of all their efforts; and now the Bible is placed in every school, and every teacher is required to spend from one to two hours each day, in giving and enforcing instruction in all the duties of man towards his Creator, towards constituted authorities, and towards his fellow-men.

And what is the experience of our own country? Those portions of the nation, most distinguished for the general diffusion of education, are those in which moral and religious influences have been most extensively introduced into schools, and have pervaded all the institutions of society. But, in those portions of our country the increase and jealousy of religious sects, and other combining causes, have had an influence in banishing the Bible, and moral and religious influence, more and more from public schools. And now we hear the widely extended complaint, that common schools are dangerous places for children while parents, who are most regardful of the moral influences exerted upon their children, are more and more withdrawing them from what they deem such contaminating influence.

Thus, in those parts of our country which have been most moral and intelligent, the education of the lower classes is deteriorating, as it respects moral and religious restraints, while the statistics of education, coming from other parts of the nation, are most appalling. We find that in one of our smallest middle states, thirty thousand adults and children are entirely without education and without schools. In one of the largest middle states, four hundred thousand adults and children are thus destitute. In one of the best educated western states, one-third of the children are without schools; while it appears, that, in the whole nation, there are a million and a half of children, and nearly as many adults, in the same deplorable ignorance, and without any means of instruction. At the same time, thousands and thousands of degraded foreigners, and their ignorant families, are pouring into this nation at every avenue. All these ignorant native and foreign adults are now voters, and have a share in the government of the nation. All these million children, in a very few years, will take the same stand; while other millions, as ignorant and destitute are hastening in their rear. What is the end of these things to be? How long will it take, at this rate, for the majority of votes, and of the physical force of the nation, to be in the hands of ignorance and vice? That terrific crisis is now before us; and a few years will witness its consummation, unless such energetic and persevering efforts are made as time never saw.

Here, we have no despotic monarch to endow seminaries for teachers, and to send every child in the nation to school for seven successive years, to place a Bible in every school, and enforce a system of moral and religious instruction. It is the people who must voluntarily do it, or it will remain undone. Public sentiment must be aroused to a sense of danger; the wealthy and intelligent must pour out their treasures to endow seminaries for teachers; moral and religious education, and the best methods of governing and regulating the human mind, must become a science; those who have had most experience, and are best qualified in this department, must be called upon to contribute their experience and combined efforts, to qualify others for these duties; men of talent and piety must enter this as the noblest and most important missionary field; females who have time and talents, must be called to aid in the effort; seminaries for teachers, with their model schools, must be established in every state; agents must be employed to arouse and enlighten the people; and, when the people are sufficiently awake to the subject, legislative and national aid must be sought.

The object aimed at is one immense and difficult enough to demand the highest exercise of every energy, and every mode of influence. If Prussia, with her dense population, finds one teacher for every ten children needful, the sparseness of population in our wide territories surely demands an equal supply. At this rate, *ninety thousand* teachers are this moment wanted to supply the destitute; and to these must be added every year *twelve thousand,* simply to meet the increase of population. But if we allow thirty pupils as the average number for every teacher, then we need *thirty thousand* teachers for present wants, and an annual addition of *four thousand* for increase of population. And yet, what has been done—what is now doing—to meet this enormous demand? While Prussia, for years, has been pouring out her well educated teachers from her forty-five seminaries, at the rate of one for every ten pupils; while France is organizing her Normal schools in all her departments for the education of her teachers; what is done in America,—wealthy, intelligent, and free

America,—whose very existence is depending on the virtuous education of her children? In New England, we hear of one solitary institution for the preparation of teachers; and, in New York, eight are just starting into being; and this is all! Now, at this moment, we need at least thirty thousand teachers, and four thousand every year in addition, just to supply the increase of youthful population. . . .

When we consider, the claims of the learned professions, the excitement and profits of commerce, manufactures, agriculture, and the arts; when we consider the aversion of most men to the sedentary, confining, and toilsome duties of teaching and governing young children; when we consider the scanty pittance that is allowed to the majority of teachers; and that few men will enter a business that will not support a family, when there are multitudes of other employments that will afford competence, and lead to wealth; it is chimerical to hope that the supply of such immense deficiencies in our national education is to come chiefly from that sex. It is woman, fitted by disposition, and habits, and circumstances, for such duties, who, to a very wide extent, must aid in educating the childhood and youth of this nation; and therefore it is, that females must be trained and educated for this employment. And, most happily, it is true, that the education necessary to fit a woman to be a teacher, is exactly the one that best fits her for that domestic relation she is primarily designed to fill.

But how is this vast undertaking to be accomplished? How can such a multitude of female teachers as are needed, be secured and fitted for such duties? The following will show how it *can* be done, if those most interested and obligated shall only *will* to have it done.

Men of patriotism and benevolence can commence by endowing two or three seminaries for female teachers in the most important stations in the nation, while to each of these seminaries shall be attached a model school, supported by the children of the place where it is located. In these seminaries can be collected those who have the highest estimate of the value of moral and religious influence, and the most talents and experience for both intellectual and moral education.

When these teachers shall have succeeded in training classes of teachers on the best system their united wisdom can devise, there will be instructors prepared for other seminaries for teachers, to be organized and conducted on the same plan; and thus a regular and systematic course of education can be disseminated through the nation.

Meantime, proper efforts being made by means of

the press, the pulpit, and influential men employed as agents for this object, the interest of the whole nation can be aroused, and every benevolent and every pious female in the nation, who has the time and qualifications necessary, can be enlisted to consecrate at least a certain number of years to this object. There is not a village in this nation that cannot furnish its one, two, three, and in some cases ten or even twenty, laborers for this field.

And, as a system of right moral and religious education gains its appropriate influence, as women are more and more educated to understand and value the importance of their influence in society, and their peculiar duties, more young females will pursue their education with the expectation that, unless paramount private duties forbid, they are to employ their time and talents in the duties of a teacher, until they assume the responsibilities of domestic life. Females will cease to feel that they are educated just to enjoy themselves in future life, and realize the obligations imposed by Heaven to live to do good. And, when females are educated as they ought to be, every woman at the close of her school education, will be well qualified to act as a teacher.

We need institutions endowed at public expense, and so constituted, that, while those who are able shall pay the full value of their privileges, those who have not the ability shall be furnished gratuitously with what they cannot purchase; while all who receive these advantages shall consider themselves pledged to devote themselves to the cause of education, and also to refund their expenses, whenever future earnings, or a change in their situation, will enable them to do it. And if men of wealth will furnish the means, if they will collect the talent and experience that are ready to engage in the enterprise, they will soon find multitudes of laborers hastening to the field. As things now are, few females of discretion and good sense would attempt, unaided, what their friends, and most of the community, would deem the Quixotic enterprise of preparing themselves to be teachers, and then set out to seek a situation in the destitute portions of our country. But let benevolent men unite in endowing institutions for those who are unprepared, and secure some organization of suitable persons, whose business it shall be to provide places for those who are prepared; let statistics of the wants of the county be sent abroad, and the cry go forth "Whom shall we send, and who will go for us?" and from amid the green hills and white villages of New England, hundreds of voices would respond, "Here am I, send me;" while kindred voices, through the whole length of the land, would echo the reply.

In behalf of such then it is, that the writer would

address this intelligent and patriotic assembly, and through them the benevolent and philanthropic of the nation: Give us the opportunity of aiding to preserve the interests and institutions of our country. . . .

AN ADDRESS ON FEMALE SUFFRAGE

In the following address delivered in the Music Hall of Boston in 1870, Miss Beecher expresses with vigor her conviction that the Creator has assigned to men and women widely different spheres. These require thoroughly differentiated schemes of education in separate higher institutions. She heartily disapproves of two tendencies of her own day, *viz.,* the movement to open higher institutions for men to young women; and the growing emphasis on a purely intellectual education for women. Believing as she does that the duties of women are "quite as difficult and important" as those of men, she would give her sex a thorough preparation for those duties in endowed schools on the college or university plan. Miss Beecher's opposition to the woman suffrage movement, together with her profound disapproval of women's entering the industrial and business world, reveal that with all her fine ardor for the improvement of women's education she was out of touch with two of the most significant tendencies of her age.

I appear this evening to present the views of that large portion of my sex who are opposed to such a change of our laws and customs as would place the responsibility of civil government on woman.

This may be done without impugning the motives, or the character, or the measures of that respectable party who hold the contrary position. As in the physical universe the nicely-balanced *centripetal* and *centrifugal* forces hold in steady curve every brilliant orbit, so, in the moral world, the radical element, which would forsake the beaten path of ages, is held in safe and steady course by the conservative; while that, also, is preserved from dangerous torpor by the antagonistic power.

And so, while claiming to represent the conservative element, I meet with respect and kindness my centrifugal friend.

First, let me state the points in which we agree, that we may more clearly appreciate those in which we differ.

We agree, then, on the general principle, that woman's happiness and usefulness are equal in value to those of man's and, consequently, that she has a right to equal advantages for securing them.

We agree, also, that woman, even in our own age and country, has never been allowed such equal advantages, and that multiplied wrongs and suffering have resulted from this injustice.

Finally, we agree that it is the right and the duty of every woman to employ the power of organization and agitation, in order to gain those advantages which are given to the one sex, and unjustly withheld from the other. . . .

At the commencement of this discussion, it was stated that the parties at issue agree in these general principles, namely, that woman's usefulness and happiness are equal in value to man's, and consequently that she has a right to equal advantages for gaining them; that she is unjustly deprived of such equal advantages, and that organization and agitation to gain them is her privilege and duty.

The points of difference are as to the nature of the advantages of which she is deprived, the consequent evils, and the mode of remedy. One party regard woman's seclusion from the professions, the universities, and the civil offices of men as the leading injustice from which most of the evils complained of are the result, and that the gift of the ballot will prove the panacea for all these wrongs. The other party believe the chief cause of evils which both are striving to remedy is the want of a just appreciation of woman's profession, and the want of such a liberal and practical training for its duties as men secure for their most honored professions.

Here we again may refer to a patent maxim of common sense, which is this: that the more difficult and important are any duties, the more scientific care and training should be bestowed on those who are to perform them. It has been in obedience to this maxim that, in Christian countries, the highest advantages have been given to those men who have charge of the spiritual and eternal interests of our race. Most of the universities of Europe and of this country were founded to educate the clergy. Next came the training of those who administer laws, and then of those who cure the sick. These are named the *liberal professions,* because society has most liberally provided for the scientific training of those who perform these duties.

That women need as much and even more scientific and practical training for their appropriate business than men, arises from the fact that they must perform duties quite as difficult and important, and a much greater variety of them. A man usually selects one branch of business for a son, and, after his school education, secures an apprenticeship of years to perfect his practical skill; and thus a success is attained which would be impossible were he to practice various trades and professions.

Now let us notice the various and difficult duties that are demanded of woman in her ordinary relations as wife, mother, housekeeper, and the mistress of servants.

First, she has charge of the economies of the family state; for, as the general rule, men are to earn the support and women administer these earnings. In this must be included the style in which a house shall be prepared and furnished, so as best to secure pure air, sunlight, and the best arrangement and conveniences for labor. If women were scientifically trained in this particular, their influence would have saved much labor and much expense. . . .

There is no department of domestic economy where there is more enormous waste than in the selection and management of fuel. Much science is involved in learning what fuel is made of; what kinds best furnish warmth without waste; what methods waste heat; what methods preserve it; what spreads it equally; what creates draughts and thus colds and headaches, and many other connected subjects. Having devoted more than usual attention to this topic, and especially to the proper selection and management of furnaces and cookstoves, it is my firm belief that if I could impart to the housekeepers of our country the knowledge I have gained, and that without any help from scientific schools, it would enable them to save millions of money and an enormous amount of ill health and discomfort.

Again, a housekeeper has charge of the selection and preparation of the food on which family health and enjoyment so much depend. To prepare her for this duty she should be taught what kinds of food are most healthful and nutritious; what kinds are best for the young and what for the aged; how each should be cooked to secure most nutriment and least waste; the relative value of buying wholesale or retail; the best modes of storing food and of preserving it from vermin or decay; what dishes are at once economical, comely, and inviting and how a husband's earnings can secure the most comfort and enjoyment with the most economical outlay. A woman needs training and instruction in this department of her duties as much as her sons need similar instruction and training in agriculture or watch-making, when that is to be their profession.

Again, the mistress of a family controls the selection and making of the clothing and furniture, and will be called to decide what is most suitable and economical; what stuffs wear longest; what hold colors best; what parts wear out soonest, and how they can be made to last the longest; how much is needed for each garment; and what is the proper way to cut and fit each article; what is the proper way of mending; what is the most economical and easiest mode of washing and ironing; and so on through a long list of duties that demand judgment, science, and care.

Again, the health of a family is especially a responsibility that rests upon woman. There is no such wise and needed physician as a well-instructed mother and housekeeper; not to cure—for that is the physician's part, but to prevent—disease, or stop it at the starting. Our gravest illnesses come from neglected colds, indigestion, and headaches.

Who first finds out when one is ill, and is best prepared to search for the cause? Why should not every housekeeper know the first symptoms of common illnesses, the cause and the cure? Not chiefly in the hospital or by the bedside is a well-instructed nurse needed, but by the family fireside, where she can observe the first symptoms, give early warning, and apply the simple cure. There is no technical training so valuable to a woman as that which enables her to keep the doctor out of the house, and to send for him when he is needed.

Again, to woman must be committed the charge of new-born infants—and of the mothers at the most perilous and most anxious period of life, and one demanding so much discretion, tenderness, and self-denying labor. Thousands of young, uninstructed mothers are sent out of life or made suffering invalids from their own ignorance of all they most need to know, or from the neglect or ignorance of untrained nurses.

The departments of practical life, to which the majority of women are ordained, ought to receive the honors and aid of lectures, professorships, endowments, and scientific treatment; the same as is bestowed to fit men for practical life. The care of a house, the conduct of a home, the management of children, the instruction and government of servants, are as deserving of scientific treatment and scientific professors and lectureships as are the care of farms, the management of manure and crops, and the raising and care of stock. Shall man secure for himself endowments, and professors, and lectures on stock-raising, the diseases of domestic animals, and the laws by which they are preserved in health, and woman be denied equal advantages for learning the laws by which health, beauty, and mental soundness may be secured to the more precious children under her care?

It is granted by all parties that it is women who are to nurse and train the children the first years of life, and they must do it either ignorantly and blunderingly, or intelligently guided by scientific knowledge. For this reason every college and high-school for women should have a well-instructed woman professor, whose duty it shall be to instruct young women (in the last years of their education) in all they need to know as wife, mother, nurse, and guardian of infancy and childhood.

For young men we find endowed scientific schools to teach them agricultural chemistry, that they may learn wisely to conduct a farm; why should not women be taught domestic chemistry and domestic philosophy? The more civilization advances, the more do complicated contrivances multiply for the charge of which women are mainly responsible. The laws that regulate heat, as applied in the construction of furnaces, stoves, ranges, and grates; the principles of hydraulics, as applied in constructing cisterns, boilers, water-pipes, faucets, and other multiplied modern conveniences, demand scientific and intelligent supervision impossible to a woman untrained in this department of her domestic duties.

Again, young men are provided with lectures on political economy, while domestic economy, as yet, has not been so honored. Most women come to the duty of providing for a family utterly ignorant of the science of comparative values, and of the greater or less economies of the articles they are to provide and preserve.

But the most important of all the departments of a woman's profession is one for which no college or high-school for women has made any proper provision.

Woman, as mother and as teacher, is to form and guide the immortal mind. She, more than any one else, is to decide the character of her helpless children, both for this and the future eternal life. And for this, liberal provision should be made; so that no woman shall finish her education till all that science and training can do shall be bestowed to fit her for this supernal duty. . . .

In this review of the varied and complicated duties of a woman's profession, we find that she needs not only the general discipline and training for the development of mental faculties, but a special training for a far greater diversity of duties than are ever to be undertaken by men. We claim that woman's profession demands such very diverse training from the professions of the other sex that access to universities for men does not meet her most sacred necessities. A university education for woman should be as diverse from that of man's as are her duties and responsibilities. . . .

Endowments have secured to young men not only a thorough training in branches of literature and science which enlarge the mental powers, but also have served to honor and elevate several of the trades and professions to which they are devoted, so that they are now on an honorable equality with the so-called liberal professions. The scientific schools, the art schools, and the schools of technology are fast elevating many heretofore degraded professions to equal honor with law, medicine, and divinity. The more these various arts and professions are made honorable by endowments to support learned professors, the larger the number of honorable and remunerative professions are provided for young men; and, as yet, woman (with one or two exceptions) has had no such opportunities provided. To support such institutions for young men, every State in the Union has been taxed, and large grants of land made by the general government, while individual benefactions have been still more abundant. Our oldest colleges all count their endowments as valued from half a million to four and five millions each. There are now more than two hundred well endowed colleges and scientific schools for young men, supporting many hundred professors. The State of New York has twelve endowed colleges, having doubled the number in twenty years. Connecticut has three endowed colleges, and four endowed professional schools. Massachusetts has four colleges and six professional schools for young men, and other States in similar proportions.

As a contrast to this liberal provision for young men, I may be allowed to narrate some of my own experience. When I commenced my profession as teacher, the most popular boarding-schools taught little except the primary branches, though occasionally was executed by the pupils a "mourning piece," that is, an embroidered tombstone under an apparition by courtesy called a weeping willow, with a row of darkly-clad weeping friends approaching it. I was among the first to introduce what are called the higher branches. My school soon numbered over one hundred; and yet I had only one room and one assistant, while I had both to teach the higher branches and to study them myself; not having been taught them in my school days. I also had to prepare my teachers, who like myself had never been trained for these departments. And as my school rose in popularity, other schools followed the example, so that as fast as I trained reliable teachers, they were drawn off by the offers of higher salaries.

Meantime all the responsibilities, which in colleges are divided among the president, the professors, the tutors, and the treasurer, rested on me. Ten years of such complicated labor, study, and responsibility destroyed health, as it has done for multitudes of other women, who have thus toiled unaided by any of the advantages given to college teachers.

Ever since that time, I have devoted my income, strength, and time to efforts for securing professional advantages of education for my sex equal to those bestowed on men. It is over forty years that these efforts have been continued. And now, after remarkable and unexpected restoration to health, the institution I founded so many years ago is again committed to my charge.

In all this period, not a single institution has been founded which includes in its curriculum the course of practical training that prepares a woman for the complicated responsibilities I have enumerated as included in her profession. The Mount Holyoke plan does not even aim at any thing of this kind, but is only a method of economy to lessen expenditure. Vassar College has no endowment to support teachers, and so its tuition fees far exceed those of colleges for men. Nor is the industrial training of woman for her distinctive profession any part of its aim, while the largest portion of the income of that institution goes for the support of men instead of women teachers, five out of seven professors being men. And the excuse for this is, that well-trained female teachers can not be taken. But if woman had received the advantages given to men, most of these honorable and remunerative positions would have been hers. . . .

There are multitudes of women in unwomanly employments, who, if educated to the scientific duties of a nurse for young infants and their mothers, with all the advantages of high culture given to medical men, and with the social honor accorded to high culture, would be greeted in many a family, be sought as the most welcome benefactors of the family state, and take a superior position to that now given to the teachers of music, French, and drawing.

Again, there is no agent of the family state who has a more constant, daily influence on the character of childhood than the one who shares with a mother the cares of the nursery. And yet where shall we find an institution in which young women are properly trained for these sacred offices? The heir of an earthly kingdom is surrounded by the noblest and the wisest, who deem the humblest office an honor in his service. But the young heir of an immortal kingdom, whose career, not for a few earthly days, but for eternal ages, is to be decided in this life, to whom is he committed, and where and how were they trained for these supernal duties? The bogs of Ireland—the shanty tenement-houses—the plantation huts—the swarming, poverty-stricken wanderers from Europe, China, and Japan are coming to reply!

The influx of wealth, the building of expensive houses demanding many servants, and the increasing demands of social life, are changing mothers from the educational training of their own offspring to the training and care of servants; and yet, in our boarding-schools and colleges for women, how much is done to train them for such duties?

When I read the curriculum of Vassar and other female colleges, methinks their graduates by such a course as this will be as well prepared to nurse the sick, train servants, take charge of infants, and manage all departments of the family state, as they would be to make and regulate chronometers, or to build and drive steam engines.

The number of branches introduced into female schools has nearly doubled since I commenced my school, while the real advantages gained by this increase have been lessened. And as yet little or no progress has been made in preparing women for the practical duties of their profession. The expenses of most popular boarding-schools confine their advantages to the rich, who do not aim to have daughters trained to do woman's work, or to earn their own independence.

The evils that women suffer from the want of proper training for their appropriate duties, few can fully realize. The Working-Woman's Union, in New York City, reports that of the 13,000 applicants for work, not one half were qualified to any kind of work in a proper manner. The societies for aiding poor women report as their greatest embarrassment that but few can sew decently, or do any other work properly. The heads of dress-making establishments complain that few can be found who can be trusted to complete a dress properly, and say that those properly trained find abundant work and good pay. The demand for good mantua-makers in country towns is universal. In former days, plain sewing was taught in schools; but now it is banished, and mothers are too pressed with labor, or too negligent, to supply the deficiency.

In the middle classes, unmarried women and widows feel that they are an incumbrance on fathers and brothers, who, from pride or duty, feel bound to support them, and yet no openings offer for them to earn an independence. Thousands of ladies of good families and good education, with aged mothers or young children to support, can find either no employments or those offering starvation wages. The school or the boarding-house is the chief alternative for such persons; and yet every opening for a school-teacher has scores, and sometimes hundreds of applicants.

The factory-girls, and those in shops and stores, must stand six, eight, or ten hours a day in bad air and unwholesome labor. The influx of ignorant and uncleanly foreigners into our kitchens, and the exactions of thriftless young housekeepers from boarding-schools, drive self-respecting American women from many of our kitchens.

Meantime, in our more wealthy classes, those who have generous and elevated aspirations feel that they have no object in life—no profession, like their brothers, by which they can secure their own independence, and aid in elevating others. Our young girls are trained only for marriage; and when that fails, fathers and brothers forbid their earning an independence, as implying disgrace to themselves.

The remedy for all this would soon be achieved were woman's work elevated to an honorable and remunerative science and profession, by the same methods that men have taken to elevate their various professions. The establishment of Woman's Universities, in which every girl shall secure as good a literary training as her brothers, and then be trained to some profession adapted to her taste and capacity, by which she can establish a home of her own, and secure an independent income— this is what every woman may justly claim and labor for, as the shortest, surest, and safest mode of securing her own highest usefulness and happiness, and that of her sex; a mode which demands only what, if once achieved as practicable, every intelligent and benevolent man would approve and delight to promote. . . .

A Woman's University, that will realize the ideal aimed at, may, perhaps, come by no sudden growth, but by many experiments in different fields and diverse departments, each aiding to advance every other, till all eventually will be combined in a harmonious and perfected result. And for this consummation my good friend and opponent is as ready to labor as those of us who have not her courage and hopes as to the results of woman suffrage.

I stated that I have resumed the charge of the seminary I founded forty years ago, to teach the higher branches, with Mrs. Stowe, then, as now, my associate. We began when women were trained to domestic labor, and almost nothing else. We have seen the pendulum swing to the other extreme, till, both in families and schools, women are taught the higher branches, and almost nothing else. We now begin at the other end, and, by the aid and counsel of the judicious women of Hartford, we hope to set an example of a woman's university which shall combine the highest intellectual culture with the highest practical skill in all the distinctive duties of womanhood. . . .

I regard the effort to introduce women into colleges for young men as very undesirable, and for many reasons. That the two sexes should be united, both as teachers and pupils, in the same institution seems very desirable, but rarely in early life by a method that removes them from parental watch and care, and the protecting influences of a home. . . .

Can woman's distinctive profession be made a large portion of her school education?

To aid in deciding these questions, the following is given as the ideal at which I have been aiming in efforts to establish a Woman's University; by which I mean, not a large boarding-establishment of pupils removed from parental care, but an institution embracing the whole course of a woman's training from infancy to a self-supporting profession, in which both parents and teachers have a united influence and agency.

According to this ideal, such an institution would be divided into distinct schools; all under the same board of supervision, and all carrying out a connected and appropriate portion of the same plan. These are:

1. The Kindergarten, for the youngest children, who are not to use books;

2. The Primary School, for children just commencing the use of books;

3. The Preparatory School, introductory to the higher;

4. The Collegiate School, embracing a course of four years;

5. The Professional School, to prepare a woman for all domestic duties and for a self-supporting profession.

For the control of all these there would be such a division of responsibilities as follows:

1. The first would be the department of intellectual training; committed to a woman of high culture in every branch taught in the collegiate school; possessing

quick discernment, intellectual and moral force, and great interest in her special department. . . .

2. The department of moral training would be given to a woman of high moral and mental culture, whose tastes, talents, and experience prepare her to excel in this department. It would be her duty to study the character and discover the excellences of every pupil, by aid both of the other teachers and the parents, and then to devise methods of improvement; instructing the other teachers how to aid in these efforts. She also would seek the aid and cooperation of the most mature and influential pupils, and direct them how to exert a cooperating influence. The general religious instruction of the institution also would be conducted under her supervision and control.

3. The department of the physical training of all the institution would be committed to a woman of good practical common sense, of refined culture and manners, and one expressly educated for this department. By the aid of both parents and teachers, she would study the constitution and habits of every pupil, and administer a method of training to develop healthfully every organ and function, and to remedy every defect in habits, person, voice, movements, and manners.

Here I would remark that my extensive investigations in many health-establishments as to the causes of the decay of female health, and my extensive opportunities for gaining the opinions and counsels of all the most learned and successful physicians of all schools, lead me to the belief that there are few chronic maladies, deformities, or unhealthful habits that may not be entirely remedied by a system of physical exercise and training in schools, under the charge of a woman properly qualified for these duties. . . .

In regard to the course of study in the collegiate department of a woman's university, there should be as great an amount as is required in any of our colleges, yet only a few studies carried to so great an extent as in many sciences pursued by men. But there should be a much greater variety, together with an accuracy and thoroughness that colleges rarely secure. And all should have reference to women's profession, and not to the professions of men. Much in this department at first must be experimental, having in view the ideal indicated.

So in regard to introducing practical training for woman's domestic duties as a part of common school education; although it is certain that much more can be done than ever has been attempted, and that, too, as a contribution to intellectual development rather than the reverse, this also must be a matter of experiment.

In regard to a special training in the preparatory and the collegiate schools for future self-supporting employments, much more can be done than has ever been supposed, and a few particulars will be enumerated to illustrate. Young women of affectionate disposition, good intelligence and morals, having only limited means, might be trained to become a mother's assistant in charge of a nursery, partly by the studies of the primary and preparatory schools and partly by learning the methods of the Kindergarten. Thousands of parents in all parts of our nation would offer liberal wages to young women thus trained for one of the most sacred offices of the family state.

Women of suitable social and moral character might be trained, in connection with school studies, to be superior seamstresses and mantua-makers, and thus be enabled to gain liberal wages. . . .

Women trained to fit young boys for college, in private families or in small neighborhood schools, would command very high remuneration in many quarters. Every young girl whose means will allow it ought to be prepared for this duty.

Pupils who have a decided talent for either music, drawing, or other fine arts, might have a special training for one of these professions; while those without any such tastes or aptitudes should be dissuaded from wasting time, labor, and money, as is so absurdly and widely practiced, in learning to play the piano and acquiring other accomplishments never pursued in after-life. Nine tenths of young girls thus instructed lose all they learn in a very short period.

Some pupils have fine voices and talent and taste for elocution, and such might be trained for teachers of this art or for public readings.

Some pupils have talents that prepare them to excel in authorship, and to such an appropriate and more extensive literary culture could be afforded.

The art of book-keeping and of quick and legible penmanship insures remunerative employment; and many other specialties might be enumerated in which, during school-days, a woman might be trained to a self-supporting profession. And every woman should be trained for all the duties that may in future life be demanded as wife, mother, nurse, and school-teacher, if not in the ordinary school, in a separate professional school.

When institutions are endowed to train women for all departments connected with the family state, domestic labor, now so shunned and disgraced, will become honorable, will gain liberal compensation, and will enable every woman to secure an independence in employments suited to her sex. And when this is attained, there will be few or none who will wish to enter the professions of men or take charge of civil government.

Having expressed so strongly my views in reference to large boarding-schools for both sexes, I will add some further details of my ideal for organizing a Woman's University. This has been suggested by recent interviews with some who may have much influence in managing the large funds recently bequeathed in Massachusetts for establishing institutions for women, in one case a lady having bestowed what will probably amount to nearly half a million, and in another case a gentleman has bequeathed a million and a half for this purpose.

This, I believe, is but the beginning of similar benefactions that will be provided for women in all parts of our country. There are men of wealth who have lost a dear mother, wife, or daughter, who would find comfort and pleasure in perpetuating a beloved name by an endowment that for age after age will minister to the education and refinement of women and the support and training of orphans.

In this view, it seems very important that the first endowed institutions of this kind should adopt plans that may be wisely imitated.

It seems desirable that such endowed institutions

should be placed in or so near a large town that the pupils of all the schools, except the professional one, should reside with their parents instead of congregating in a great boarding-house. The professional school would ordinarily embrace only women of maturity, and might demand a location with surrounding land for flori-culture, horticulture, and other feminine professions.

The Kindergarten, the primary school, and the pre-paratory school might each have a principal and an as-sociate principal, supported partly by tuition fees and partly by endowment. These principals might establish a family, consisting of the two, who would take the place of parents to several adopted orphans and to several pay-pupils whose parents, from ill health or other causes, would relinquish the care of their children.

The collegiate schools might have endowed depart-ments corresponding to professorships in colleges, each having a principal and associate principal, who also could establish families on the same plan. When com-pleted, the university would then consist of a central building for school purposes, surrounded by fifteen or twenty families, each having a principal and associate principal, acting as parents to a family of from ten to twelve pupils, and all in some department of domestic training.

Thus some thirty or forty ladies of high character and

culture would be provided with the independence and advantages now exclusively bestowed on men, while at the same time the institution would practically and to a considerable extent be an orphan asylum offering unusual advantages.

In regard to the practicability of finding women properly qualified to carry on such a university with success, there is no difficulty. Few know so well as I do how many women of benevolence and high culture are living with half their noblest energies unemployed for want of the opportunities and facilities provided for men. There is nothing needed but endowments to secure the services of a large number of ladies of the highest culture and moral worth, well qualified to establish not only one but many such institutions.

LETTERS TO THE PEOPLE ON HEALTH AND HAPPINESS (1856)

Perhaps none of Catherine Beecher's numerous writings was more influential than those in which she described the sickly condition of a large proportion of American women and children and urged a well-planned system of physical exercises, together with more out-of-door activities to overcome this evil. Miss Beecher's textbooks in physiology and calisthenics had a wide distribution and played their part in opening the minds of the American people to the need of physical training and health education in the schools.

LETTER FIRST

MY FRIENDS:

Will you let me come to you in your work-shop, or office, or store, or study? and you, my female friends, may I enter your nursery, your parlor, or your kitchen? I have matters of interest to present in which every one of you has a deep personal concern.

215

I have facts to communicate, that will prove that the American people are pursuing a course, in their own habits and practices, which is destroying health and happiness to an extent that is perfectly appalling. Nay more, I think I shall be able to show, that the majority of parents in this nation are systematically educating the rising generation to be feeble, deformed, homely, sickly, and miserable; as much so as if it were their express aim to commit so monstrous a folly.

I think I can show also, that if a plan for *destroying female health,* in all the ways in which it could be most effectively done, were drawn up, it would be exactly the course which is now pursued by a large portion of this nation, especially in the more wealthy classes.

At the same time, I can present *facts* showing that the results of such a course have been an amount of domestic unhappiness and of individual suffering in all classes in our land that is perfectly frightful, and that these dreadful evils are constantly increasing.

You have read often of the Greeks. Some twenty centuries ago they were a small people, in a small country; and yet they became the wisest and most powerful of all nations, and thus conquered nearly the whole world. And they were remarkable not only for their wisdom and strength, but for their great beauty, so that the statues they made to resemble their own men and women have, ever since, been regarded as the most perfect forms of human beauty.

The chief reason why they excelled all nations in these respects, was the great care they took in educating their children. They had two kinds of schools—the one to train the minds, and the other to train the bodies of their children. And though they estimated very highly the education of the mind, they still more valued that part of school training which tended to develop and perfect the body. . . .

But the American people have pursued a very different course. It is true that a large portion of them have provided schools for educating the minds of their children; but instead of providing teachers to train the bodies of their offspring, most of them have not only entirely neglected it, but have done almost every thing they could do to train their children to become feeble, sickly, and ugly. And those, who have not pursued so foolish a course, have taken very little pains to secure the proper education of the body for their offspring during the period of their school life.

In consequence of this dreadful neglect and mismanagement, the children of this country are every year becoming less and less healthful and good-looking. There is a great change in reference to this matter within my memory. When young, I noticed in my travels the children in school-houses, or on Sunday in the churches, almost all of them had rosy cheeks, and looked full of health and spirits. But now, when I notice the children in churches and schools, both in city and country, a great portion of them either have sallow or pale complexions, or look delicate or partially misformed.

When I was young, I did not know of any sickly children. All my brothers and sisters and young playmates could go out in all weathers, were not harmed by wetting their feet, would play on the snow and ice for hours without cloaks or shawls, and never seemed to be troubled with the cold. And the tender parents of these days would be shocked to see how little clothing we wore in the bitterest cold of winter.

But now, though parents take far more pains to wrap up their little ones, to save them from the cold and wet, the children grow less and less healthy every year. And I rarely find a school-room full of such rosy-cheeked, strong, fine-looking children as I used to see thirty years ago.

Every year I hear more and more complaints of the poor health that is so very common among grown people, especially among women. And physicians say, that this is an evil that is constantly increasing, so that they fear, ere long, there will be no healthy women in the country.

At the same time, among all classes of our land, we are constantly hearing of the superior health and activity of our ancestors. Their physical health and strength, and their power of labor and endurance, was altogether beyond any thing witnessed in the present generation.

Travelers, when they go to other countries, especially when they visit England, from whence our ancestors came, are struck with the contrast between the appearance of American women and those of other countries in the matter of health. In this nation, it is rare to see a married woman of thirty or forty, especially in the more wealthy classes, who retains the fullness of person and freshness of complexion that mark good health. But in England, almost all the women are in the full perfection of womanhood at that period of life.

Now it is a fact, that the health of children depends very much on the health of their parents. Feeble and sickly fathers and mothers seldom have strong and healthy children. And when one parent is well and the other sickly, then a part of the children will be sickly and a part healthy.

Thus the more parents become unhealthy the more feeble children will be born. And when these feeble children grow up and become parents, they will have a still more puny and degenerate offspring. So the case will go on, from bad to worse, with every generation.

What then, if what I state be true, are the prospects of this nation, unless some great and radical change is effected?

Such a change is possible. The American people have far better advantages than the Greeks had to train their offspring to be strong, healthful, and beautiful, while the means of *retrieving* the mischief already done are in their hands. Nothing is needed but a *full knowledge* of the case, and then the *application of that practical common-sense and efficiency to this object,* which secures to them such wonderful success in all their business affairs. It is with the hope of doing something to effect such a change that this book has been prepared.

I have been led to this effort by many powerful influences. More than half of the mature years of my own life have been those of restless debility and infirmities, that all would have been saved by the knowledge contained in this work. . . .

It is impossible that the evils referred to should be remedied until they are known, and their causes fully understood. And it is impossible to make them comprehended except by giving clear ideas of the construction of certain portions of the human body, the end designed by these organs, and the methods for securing these ends. This is what is first proposed in this work;

and in attempting it, the aim will be to avoid all that is not strictly practical, and all the technics of science that are needless. It also will be the aim to write in so clear and simple a style that even children can understand every sentence; and to make the work so *short,* that even American *men of business* can be induced to read it.

The following is an outline of the plan:

The first part contains a brief description of certain organs of the human body most important to health and happiness, and which are most injured and abused by the American people.

The second part shows what is the proper treatment of these organs in order to secure the most perfect health and physical happiness.

The third part points out the various methods in which these organs are most frequently injured.

Part fourth shows the many evil results of such abuse and mismanagement.

Part fifth points out the remedies for these evils.

In regard to the first portion, it is feared that some who are familiar with physiology may pass it over. This is earnestly deprecated. All that follows is so intimately connected with the first part, that none of the work can be fully appreciated after such an omission.

It is a very small book; it will not take over two or three hours to read it.

I beseech you for your own sake, for the sake of all you love best, to read *the whole*. . . . .

CALISTHENICS

This word is pronounced Calis-then-ics. It is formed by the two Greek words *kalos,* signifying *beautiful,* and *sthenos,* signifying *strength.*

It is the name of a course of exercises designed to promote health, and thus to secure beauty and strength.

Gymnastics, also, are exercises designed to secure health and strength. They ordinarily are more severe than this course, while they require apparatus, and a room set apart for the purpose.

The following are the distinctive advantages offered:

1. This system can be practiced in schools of every description, in the family, in nurseries, in hospitals, and in health establishments, *without apparatus,* and *without a room set apart for the purpose.*

2. It excludes all those severe exercises that involve danger, either from *excess* or from *accidents.* It is maintained that many athletic exercises suited to the stronger sex are not suited to the female constitution. This is a system that contains all that either sex needs for the *perfect development* of the body. Any more severe ex-

ercises are useful only for men whose professions require some unusual physical strength or endurance. This method is adapted to mixed schools, so that both sexes can perform them together.

3. This system is arranged on *scientific principles,* with the design of exercising *all* the muscles, and of exercising them *equably* and *harmoniously.* It embraces most of what is to be found in the French and English works that exhibit the system of *Ling,* the celebrated Swedish Professor, whose method has been widely adopted in European schools and universities.

It also contains, in addition, many valuable exercises that have been employed in Health Establishments for the cure of disease and deformities.

4. This system is so illustrated by drawings, and so exactly arranged as to mode and time, that *any* person, young or old, can practice it without aid from a teacher, and in any place. The members of a family in the parlor, the children in the nursery, the invalid in the chamber, the seamstress and milliner in their shops, the student or professional man in his office, study, or counting-room, can open a window twice or thrice a day, and have all the "fresh air and exercise" needed for *perfect health,* by simply following the directions in this work. In the Introduction to the Calisthenics will be found the benefits to be hoped from the practice of these exercises.

CATHERINE BEECHER

Suggestions to Teachers in Using This Work

The two grand causes of the ill health and physical deterioration so common are, first, a want of *knowledge* of the construction of the body and the laws of health; and, next, a want of *thought* and *conscience* on the subject.

Multitudes abuse their bodies because they do not know the mischiefs they are perpetrating.

Perhaps as many more go on in courses that they know to be injurious, because these matters are never urged on their attention and conscience as matters of *duty*. All the strong motives of religion and of the eternal world are brought to bear, from the pulpit and at the Sunday-school, to enforce certain duties that are no more important to the best interests of man than those "laws of health" which are so widely disregarded. And yet they are as truly the "laws of God" as any that were inscribed by his finger on tables of stone.

What is needed, then, in every school, is "line upon line, precept upon precept," urged *daily* on the attention and conscience of the young. For this purpose it ought to be the *official* duty of one person to take charge of all that relates to the health and physical training of every collection of the young for education. It is hoped that a time is at hand when *endowments* will be provided to secure this object, as they now are furnished almost exclusively for the training of the intellectual powers.

The teacher who has charge of the Health Department might give out one lesson a week from this book to the whole school. This should be preceded by a familiar lecture on the subject, *illustrated by specimens.* The most important bones of the body, the windpipe and lungs of some animal, which can be obtained at some market, together with models, drawings, and manikins, should all be presented, to make the lecture interesting and lucid. After such a lecture the youngest child in school could study any lesson in this work intelligently and with interest.

PART III

MARY LYON

Life of Mary Lyon.
New England Female Seminary for Teachers.
Mount Holyoke Female Seminary.
Principles and Design of the Mount Holyoke Female
Seminary.

MARY LYON

(Facing Page 228)

MARY LYON, PATHFINDER OF COLLEGE EDUCATION FOR WOMEN

OF THE three early American pioneers of women's education, all born or educated in New England, it may be said of Mary Lyon that she was most truly a daughter of the Puritans. Reared in the deeply religious atmosphere of a small farming community in western Massachusetts, she maintained, as a recent biographer has said of her, a "strictly Biblical" attitude toward the world. It is significant that a friend should have remarked years after her death that Mary Lyon's life was "an added verse to Hebrews XI"—the chapter beginning "Now faith is the substance of things hoped for, the evidence of things not seen." [1] Imbued with intense religious convictions and enthusiasms, Mary Lyon's labors in behalf of the higher education of women partook of the nature of a religious crusade. Not only did

[1] See HOWE, M. A. DE WOLFE, *Classic Shades: Five Leaders of Learning and Their Colleges*, p. 44, Little, Brown & Co., Boston, 1928.

she believe that the Lord of Hosts was on her side in the struggle to lift women's schooling above the level of the three R's, but the type of advanced education for her sex which she envisaged was designed to win converts to religion and recruits for the mission fields of the East. The Puritan temper of the founder of Mount Holyoke was shown not only in her ardent Calvinistic faith; it revealed itself as well in a heart-searching analysis of her own motives and impulses in the light of duty. In her last religious address to her students, Mary Lyon made this revealing statement which is carved upon her tomb: "There is nothing in the universe that I fear, but that I shall not know all my duty or fail to do it." There speaks a true spiritual descendant of Cotton Mather and all his earnest Puritan brotherhood.

Mary Lyon was born in Buckland, Franklin County, in the hills of western Massachusetts, February 28, 1797. As the fifth of seven children of a humble farmer, she was called upon to work hard from her early childhood. Her educational advantages were those offered by the district school of her town and were meager indeed. Yet from the first years of her schooling this vigorous country girl, trained to endure hardships, to labor long hours, and to rely upon herself, showed an eager craving for knowledge and a zeal in acquiring it that resulted in her outstripping all her fellow pupils. She seems to have had a remarkable memory and unusual powers of thought and understanding. One of her biographers quotes the Rev. Joseph Emerson, principal of Byfield Academy, where Miss Lyon was later a pupil, as saying that he had instructed several young ladies whose minds were better disciplined than hers but in sheer mental power Mary Lyon was superior to any other pupil he had ever had in his seminary.[1]

In 1810 Mary's mother, who had been left a widow several years before, remarried and left the family homestead taking the younger children with her. Mary, then thirteen years old, remained with an older brother for whom she kept house so efficiently that he paid her a dollar a week to assist her in her studies. In the intervals of work she attended school, gleaning what enlightenment she could, until she was seventeen years of age. Then began her teaching career in a school

[1] HITCHCOCK, EDWARD, *The Power of Christian Benevolence Illustrated in the Life and Labors of Mary Lyon,* p. 16, third edition, Hopkins, Bridgman and Co., Northampton, 1852.

near Shelburne Falls, Massachusetts. Although she devoted all her powers generously to her work, she was paid but seventy-five cents a week and "boarded round" among the parents of her pupils, as was customary. With the pittance she was able to save, she went to Sanderson Academy in the neighboring town of Ashfield for several scattered terms, studying with an eagerness and zeal that soon attracted the attention of her teachers. Indeed one of her instructors said of her: "She is all intellect; she does not know that she has a body to care for." [1] Clad in a coarse dress, spun and woven at home and gathered up clumsily at neck and waist, this sturdy, rather uncouth country girl, consumed with a desire to learn, had little concern with matters of dress and social behavior.

Fortunately for Miss Lyon at this stage of her life, she became the fast friend of Miss Amanda White, one of the students in the seminary, whose father, Squire White, was a trustee of the institution. Owing to her friend's influence she was taken into the Whites' comfortable home and under their friendly guidance learned many useful lessons in the amenities of man-

[1] PIERCE, B. K., "Mary Lyon and Her Seminary," *The National Repository,* p. 121, February, 1877.

ners and dress. Moreover, when her scanty funds quite gave out, the trustees of the academy, impressed by her ability and earnestness, granted her free tuition.

In 1821 a piece of real good fortune came to Miss Lyon. Amanda White was to be sent to Byfield Academy, a superior school in the eastern part of the state, and Squire White made it possible for Miss Lyon to accompany her friend. Years afterward the founder of Mount Holyoke once described the journey to her pupils:

"You can hardly understand, young ladies, what a great thing it was to get to Byfield. It was almost like going to Europe now. Why, it took us *three* long days to go from Ashfield to Byfield. Good Esq. White, who was one of my fathers, took me in his own carriage with his daughter." [1]

Byfield seems to have made a deep and abiding impression upon the mind and character of Miss Lyon. Under the able and sympathetic guidance of Rev. Joseph Emerson her mental powers were developed and disciplined. Owing to his dynamic influence, also, her

---

[1] Fisk, Fidelia, *Recollections of Mary Lyon* . . . , pp. 45–46, Boston, American Tract Society, 1866.

religious life became far deeper and more intense. For the remainder of her life the Bible was to be for Mary Lyon a fountain-head of wisdom and inspiration. Furthermore, one of her former pupils has declared that Miss Lyon learned to agree with Mr. Emerson that the station of woman "is designed by Providence to be subordinate and dependent, to a degree far exceeding the difference in native talents."[1] Certain it is that in later years she took little interest in the movement to secure larger rights for women, and believed that women's duties should be "retired and private," her labors "modest and unobtrusive."

A further influence that may be traced to Byfield was the growing realization in Miss Lyon's thought of the true purpose of education as increasing the individual's social usefulness. At Byfield, too, she became more deeply impressed with the unequal educational advantages of men and women and the great need of securing a broader intellectual and moral training for her sex.

In the autumn of 1821, after an all too short period of study at Byfield, Miss Lyon returned to Ashfield to

[1] FISK, FIDELIA, op. cit., p. 48.

teach in the academy where a year before she had been a student. But she was not permitted to remain there long. In Byfield Academy she had formed a deep and lasting friendship with one of the young women teaching there, Zilpah P. Grant. Miss Grant invited her to be her assistant in the Adams Female Academy, Londonderry, New Hampshire, and Miss Lyon gladly accepted the offer. The academy was not open in the winter—a general custom—so Miss Lyon spent her long winter vacations at home in Buckland instructing a class of young women who wished to become teachers. As many of her pupils were very poor, she did her utmost to keep the tuition rates low. It was in this winter school that Miss Lyon began the practice, later continued at Mount Holyoke, of giving earnest religious instruction to her pupils. Indeed her religious work, no less than her teaching of advanced studies, helped to draw much attention to her school in the western part of the state.

After six years had passed, Miss Lyon reluctantly left Buckland to devote herself to the new seminary at Ipswich, of which Miss Grant had just been made the head. In a short time Ipswich Academy became one of the most popular and renowned boarding schools in New England. Because of the popularity of the school and of the fact that the applicants for admission exceeded the accommodations, Miss Grant and Miss Lyon decided to refuse admission to all girls under fourteen years, and to require more solid qualifications for enrollment. Despite these restrictions 198 girls were admitted in 1831, the students coming from nearly every state of the Union. The Seminary offered them a thorough English education without foreign languages, music, or the customary feminine courses in needle-work.

Before her acceptance of the headship of the Ipswich school, Miss Grant had been informed by the trustees that it was their intention to make the academy a permanent institution of high standards. This prospect appealed powerfully to Miss Grant, since even before coming to Ipswich she had become deeply interested in the plan of an endowed seminary for women which should offer to them an education not inferior to the college education of men. If her loyal friend and biographer Dr. Hitchcock is to be believed, Miss Lyon was not at first greatly interested in her friend's scheme, and it was not until about 1830 that she "warmed to the prospect." [1] By that time, however, she had become profoundly concerned with the problem of how to furnish generous educational opportunities, not to girls of the well-to-do middle class, but to the daughters of poor farmers and artisans who, like herself, were struggling to gain an education against discouraging odds. Slowly in the years from 1824 to 1830 the resolve took root in her mind to secure for young women of the poorer classes in Massachusetts an education as broad and thorough as that furnished to their brothers in the colleges of the state. It was not long before she perceived that such an education could only be secured by means of an adequately endowed seminary. Thus Mary Lyon, traversing the same path that had been trodden before her by Emma Willard and Catherine Beecher, attained the same broad outlook upon her problem: the higher education of women was not possible without a solid economic foundation.

Because of her underlying belief that the aim of women's education was to make them better wives, mothers, and teachers and above all more helpful com-

[1] HITCHCOCK, EDWARD, *op. cit.,* p. 159.

panions of men in their religious work, Miss Lyon at first seems to have harbored the plan of a large seminary for women built and endowed by the church. It was only after she became convinced that the majority of ministers were as doubtful of the expediency of bestowing a solid higher education upon poor women as was the general public that she abandoned this hope.

The years between 1830 and 1834 were restless ones for Mary Lyon. During this period she was torn between her wish to stand faithfully by her friend at Ipswich and her eager desire to embark upon her cherished project. Her letters at this time reveal how long and difficult was her struggle. But in 1834 the resolve had crystallized to leave Ipswich and venture on the great undertaking of her life. Even before the outset of her enterprise, she had become convinced that she could do little to realize her dream of a higher seminary for poor young women unless she could enlist the interest of men of social position and influence. Well she knew that public opinion in the 1830's would not tolerate platform addresses or social prominence on the part of women, no matter how worthy might be the cause they had espoused. Therefore she wrote Miss Grant in 1833 with respect to her project: "I feel more and more that the whole business must, in name, devolve on benevolent gentlemen, and not on yourself or on myself."

Apparently her glowing faith, her enthusiastic and tireless efforts, her well-thought-out plan did in time attract the attention and arouse the active interest of influential men, including Mr. Choate of Essex, Deacon Safford of Boston, Dr. Humphrey, and Dr. Edward Hitchcock, later president of Amherst College, who had instructed her in science and was her earliest biographer.

A beginning was made in September, 1834, when a dozen gentlemen gathered in her simple parlor and listened to her outline of the scheme. At this meeting a self-perpetuating committee of clergymen and others was appointed which "stood before the public as the responsible agents for establishing the proposed seminary, until, a charter having been obtained, and trustees appointed, their services were no longer needed." [1]

Aided by the active efforts of these gentlemen, Mary Lyon embarked on the difficult business of soliciting

[1] HITCHCOCK, EDWARD, *op. cit.*, p. 201.

funds for the projected seminary. She was assisted by the Rev. Roswell Hawks, who devoted himself to awakening interest in the plan both in Massachusetts and Connecticut and in raising money for the land and building. As for Miss Lyon, she often accompanied him on his journeys, jolting along in the stage coaches of the day and seeking to interest even the passengers in her scheme. Her task it was to make a house-to-house canvass in Ipswich and other towns, eagerly explaining her plan of giving women larger educational opportunities to housewives and mothers whose own education had been scanty indeed. Nevertheless these women gave most generously of their hard-earned savings, tucked away to buy a comfortable chair or a new carpet; and it was the housewives of Ipswich who contributed the first thousand dollars. Great must have been Miss Lyon's joy when, at a meeting in Deacon Safford's house in Boston, $3,000 was pledged to the cause. A biographer refers to Miss Lyon's account books, carefully kept for several years, which show approximately $27,000 contributed by about 1,800 persons in 91 towns. As is sometimes the case, the poor seem to have given, relatively to their means, more generously than the rich. The contributions ranged in amounts from two of $1,000 each to three of six cents each.[1]

When the amounts raised appeared to justify such a forward step, a beautiful site for the new seminary was selected at South Hadley, among the hills of the Connecticut Valley, and near the old towns of Northampton and Amherst, with their libraries and atmosphere of culture. The grounds comprised fifteen acres. While the committee of men set about securing an act of incorporation, the Rev. Roswell Hawks, who had been made treasurer, and Miss Lyon continued their labors to raise funds. With dauntless faith, ground was broken for the new building before the amount necessary to finance the work had been obtained. Little by little, as the building rose, according to Miss Lyon's own plan, the money was secured to pay for it. On October 3, 1836, the corner stone was laid with religious ceremonies "amid heart-felt thanksgivings on the part of Mary Lyon, and serious misgivings on the part of other wit-

[1] HOWE, M. A. DE W., op. cit., p. 59.

nesses. . . ." [1] But nothing could dampen Miss Lyon's flaming hope. As soon as the building approached completion, she set about the task of raising funds for the furnishings, appealing not only to individuals but to churches.

Miss Lyon had announced that the new seminary would be opened on November 8, 1837, and opened it was, contrary to the belief of her less optimistic friends, although the unsettled conditions within the building might have disheartened a less ardent spirit. The accommodations provided for eighty students but more than that number presented themselves within a short time after the opening. True to her initial purpose that this school should serve the needs of young women of limited means, Miss Lyon, against the advice of the trustees, fixed the entire expense for board and tuition at sixty-four dollars a year. This policy made it necessary to call upon each student to perform at least two hours of domestic work daily. Probably most of the serious young women of the first years complied willingly with the requirement, since they well knew

[1] PIERCE, B. K., "Mary Lyon and Her Seminary," *The National Repository,* p. 123, February, 1877.

that this was a means of reducing expenses and opening the doors of educational opportunity. But Miss Lyon set other values on domestic work by the students. She believed that it tended to secure independence of domestic servants, to break down social differences, to develop family feeling, and to serve as a means of physical training. No doubt she shrewdly suspected that the rule of domestic service would serve to sift the earnest students from their more dilettante sisters—as it probably did. It is characteristic of Miss Lyon that, although burdened with the administration of the seminary and with teaching duties as well, she performed her full share of domestic work.

In the initial period of the seminary the course was restricted to three years. The earliest catalogues refer to a junior class, a middle class, and a senior class. Satisfactory completion of three years of study was rewarded by a parchment certificate which read:

A.B. has completed the prescribed course of study at the Mount Holyoke Seminary and by her attainments and correct deportment is entitled to this testimonial.

Given at South Hadley etc.

Mary Lyon, Principal

.... Secretary.[1]

[1] HITCHCOCK, EDWARD, op. cit., p. 311.

243

The catalogue of Mount Holyoke's first year shows that the course of study had not been completely organized, but the catalogue for 1838-9 contains the curriculum as definitely determined. The requirements for entering the Junior class were laid down as "an acquaintance with the general principles of English Grammar, a good knowledge of Modern Geography, Goodrich's *History of the United States,* Watts' *On the Mind,* Colburn's *First Lessons* (in arithmetic), and the whole of Adams's *New Arithmetic.*" No students were received who were not over sixteen and had not passed satisfactory examinations in these preparatory subjects. The course of study for the first or junior class is given as follows:

"Ancient Geography, Ancient and Modern History: Text books, Worcester's Elements, Goldsmith's Greece, Rome, and England, and Grimshaw's France, Day's Algebra commenced, Sullivan's Political Class Book, Hayward's Physiology, Outline of Botany, Outline of Natural Philosophy, Newman's Rhetoric, English Grammar: Murray's Grammar and Exercises, Pope's Essay on Man." [1]

[1] From the catalogue of 1838–1839.

The studies of the middle class included:

"Day's Algebra completed, Playfair's Euclid (old edition) six books, Abercrombie on the Intellectual Powers, Marsh's Ecclesiastical History, Beck's Botany commenced, Beck's chemistry, Wilkin's Astronomy, Smellie's Philosophy of Natural History, Geology, Alexander's Evidences of Christianity, English Grammar continued—Young's Night Thoughts." [1]

To cap the structure the following studies were required of the senior class:

"Playfair's Euclid, Supplement, Olmsted's Natural Philosophy, Beck's Botany continued, Paley's Natural Theology, Whately's Logic, Whately's Rhetoric, Intellectual Philosophy, Wayland's Moral Philosophy, Wayland's Political Economy, Butler's Analogy, Milton's Paradise Lost." [2]

It has seemed desirable to print these early courses of study in full as they can be found only in the first catalogues of Mount Holyoke Seminary, which are very rare, and in Hitchcock's biography, long out of print. The student of educational history will perhaps recog-

[1] *Ibid.*
[2] *Ibid.*

nize the close similarity between the initial curriculum of Mount Holyoke and that of the English and scientific course offered in certain colleges for men of the same period. The extent and variety of the sciences offered seem a little surprising for that time. On the other hand the absence of all instruction in the ancient and modern languages seems also somewhat unusual. However, the first catalogue contains the statement: "In some cases, individuals may devote a part of their time to branches not included in the regular course, (Latin for instance) and occupy a longer period in completing the studies of one class." In later years Latin and modern languages found place in the course of study and in 1862 a fourth year was added and the curriculum enriched by the inclusion of Greek.

As a judge of character and ability Miss Lyon revealed that keen and penetrating perception with which the true administrator is endowed. Associated with her in the opening year of the seminary were Eunice Caldwell, Mary Smith, and Amanda Hodgman. Later were added Abigail Moore and Mary Whitman—beloved of the students—and other able assistants. These teachers were well qualified for their work and contributed greatly to the success of the school. The salaries on which these devoted women managed to live seem to us of today a niggardly pittance. Miss Lyon herself refused to accept more than $200 a year as recompense for her services and her teachers entered into her spirit and followed her example. By means of careful management, at the close of the seminary's first year all outstanding household bills were paid and there remained a respectable sum to be turned over to the treasurer in part payment of the remaining indebtedness on the building. A new institution for the higher education of women had been auspiciously launched and had successfully navigated the rapids of its first year.

In his early sketch of the life of Mount Holyoke's founder, the Rev. Mr. Pierce emphasizes "the great central purpose" of the foundation which, he declares, was "to present to the Church and the world, as efficient Christian workers, a body of thoroughly educated and as truly consecrated, young women." [1]

From the days at Byfield Academy, when her religious nature had been profoundly stirred by the teachings and

[1] "Mary Lyon and Her Seminary," *The National Repository,* p. 126, February, 1877.

influence of the Rev. Joseph Emerson, Miss Lyon had increasingly thought of education as a means to social and religious service. Therefore it is not surprising to learn that Bible reading and study held paramount place in the curriculum at Mount Holyoke and that public and private devotions were emphasized. Miss Lyon took under her special charge the daily devotional exercises, at which the entire school was assembled. Endowed with fervid enthusiasm for religious and moral causes and with a cheerful and winning personality, Miss Lyon made these exercises deeply stirring and impressive, as several of her students testified in later years.[1] More and more she came to believe that the greatest task of her seminary was to enkindle the spiritual life of her pupils who were professed Christians and to encourage them to use every effort in the "conversion" of their fellow students who had not openly espoused Christianity. Her biographer, Rev. Mr. Pierce, writes of the intense religious interest which often captured the seminary members and describes its fruits:

"Every year of her administration remarkable religious

---

[1] See Fisk, Fidelia, *Recollections of Mary Lyon* . . . pp. 128–136, American Tract Society, Boston, 1866.

movements occurred in the Seminary often embracing nearly every unconverted student. Indeed this annual Pentecost came to be expected as one of the looked for happy events of every year; its absence an occasion of surprise and grief." [1]

During the twelve years of her administration Miss Lyon became actively interested in the work of foreign missions. She entered into vigorous correspondence with missionaries in the field and arranged for them to make addresses and hold meetings in the seminary during their furloughs at home. With the self-sacrificing zeal which so distinguished her, Miss Lyon devoted nearly half of her meager salary to missionary work and so inspired her teachers and pupils by word and example that they subscribed over one thousand dollars yearly to missions. As might be expected, many teachers and students became fired with crusading fervor and enlisted as missionaries in foreign fields, proving very efficient agents of the American Board of Missions. Others became wives of missionaries and devoted themselves to aiding the work of their husbands. Whether the yearly "Pentecosts" of religious fervor and the recurrent waves of

[1] *Op. cit.*, p. 127.

missionary enthusiasm had an adverse effect on the intellectual atmosphere of the seminary and the studious work of the students it is difficult to determine. According to Pierce the regular course of study was rarely interrupted, only when religious feeling and interest had become "absorbing." [1]

From its opening in 1837 the growth of the seminary in numbers and influence was continuous. In a period of twelve years from 1837 to 1849 the school grew from 116 pupils and four teachers to 224 pupils and sixteen teachers.[2] At the anniversary exercises held every year, a long list of eminent men made addresses, including the Reverend Lyman Beecher, Dr. Mark Hopkins, president of Williams College, and the Reverend Edward Hitchcock, president of Amherst College.

For only twelve years Mary Lyon administered the institution she had created and into which she had poured so much of herself that Mount Holyoke college has often been said to be but "the lengthened shadow" of its founder. The laborious life and many deprivations of her early years, the unselfish expenditure of all her energy

[1] *Op. cit.*, p. 126.
[2] HITCHCOCK, EDWARD, *op. cit.*, p. 314.

and thought and time without surcease of effort, which made possible the foundation and administration of a properly financed higher seminary for women, were bound to tell upon her health. Her physique weakened by incessant care and labor, she became infected with a disease contracted from a dying pupil, to whom she was giving spiritual aid and comfort, and died on March 5, 1849. On the seminary grounds her friends and former students have built a monument of white Italian marble to the memory of a fine teacher and inspirer.

The influence of Mount Holyoke in stimulating the higher education of American women has been considerable. This seminary, with its ever-rising academic standards and with its body of intelligent and socially useful alumnæ, gave to New England and other sections of the country an impressive demonstration of the social value and importance of a solidly educated womanhood. To the influence of Mary Lyon's seminary may be traced the establishment of several similar higher schools in the western states. Unquestionably the foundation of Smith and Wellesley colleges for women received stimulus from the older pioneer institution of their state. Furthermore it is probable that the missionary and educational zeal of Mary Lyon inspired the Women's Board of Foreign Missions in Boston to establish in the early seventies that High School for Girls in Constantinople which was later chartered by the state of Massachusetts as the American College for Women in Constantinople. As is true of all great spirits, the good that Mary Lyon accomplished lived and grew after her.

NEW ENGLAND FEMALE SEMINARY FOR TEACHERS [1]

The following selection is probably the first published appeal (1832) written by Miss Lyon in behalf of the seminary whose detailed plan was slowly taking form in her mind. The brief, general statements concerning the project reveal that it had not yet been completely thought through. It will be noted that there is no reference here to domestic work by the students, nor is the training of religious leaders and missionaries listed among the objects to be accomplished by the proposed seminary. Rather is the whole emphasis laid on training well-qualified teachers and on leading the way toward the establishment of "permanent female seminaries in our land."

———————

Several friends of education and of evangelical religion are considering the expediency of attempting to raise funds to found a permanent female seminary in New England.

[1] From HITCHCOCK, EDWARD, *op. cit.*, pp. 164–167.

General Object

The main object of the proposed institution will be to prepare young ladies of mature minds for active usefulness, especially to become teachers.

Character

1. Its religious character is to be strictly evangelical.
2. Its literary character is to be of a high order.

Location

This has not yet been selected. An attempt will be made to embrace as many of the following requisites as possible in the location:

1. That it be central for New England.
2. That it be surrounded by a community marked for intelligence and public spirit.
3. That a liberal proportion of the funds be raised by the town and its immediate vicinity.
4. That the particular spot be healthy and pleasant, a little removed from public business, and so situated as to be free from all other encumbrances.

Funds

The amount of funds should be sufficient to furnish the following accommodations:—

1. Several acres of land.
2. Buildings sufficiently capacious to furnish from one hundred to two hundred pupils with accommodations for school and boarding.

3. Furniture.

4. An ample library and apparatus.

DOMESTIC ARRANGEMENTS

It is proposed that the domestic department should be under the direct superintendence of such persons as are qualified for the trust. In order to give as much independence and facility to the trustees as possible, in organizing the establishment, and in order to avoid difficulties in filling offices from time to time, it is proposed that all the furniture should be owned by the corporation.

BOARDING-HOUSE

The plan which has been proposed for the buildings is suited,

1. To give to the young ladies superior privileges, both for retirement and for social intercourse, and in an eminent degree to promote health, comfort, and domestic happiness, and intellectual, moral, and religious improvement.

2. To furnish each member with a small chamber, exclusively her own.[1] The great advantages of such a

[1] This feature of the plan was not Miss Grant's, and Miss Lyon afterwards gave it up.

privilege can scarcely be realized, except by those who have often felt that they would give up almost any of their common comforts, for the sake of such retirement as can be enjoyed only in a separate apartment. To persons of reflection, the advantages will doubtless appear much greater than the extra expense, especially when it is considered that this institution is not designed for younger misses, but especially for the benefit of ladies of mature age.

FAMILY DISCIPLINE

The family discipline is to be entirely distinct from the domestic concerns. This, together with the general improvement of the pupils out of school, is to be committed directly to the teachers. The family discipline should be very systematic, but of a kind adapted to the age of its members. The whole should resemble a well-regulated voluntary association, where the officers and members are all faithful to their trust.

The plan which has been proposed for buildings is particularly suited to promote family discipline, and to render it at once easy, systematic, and pleasant to all.

1. It is such that the whole family will naturally and necessarily be arranged in a convenient number of sections, each of which can be easily directed by an appropriate head.

2. It is such as to bring all the young ladies under a direct and natural supervision. This will tend at once to secure order and propriety, and at the same time to exclude all necessity of anything like apparent watchfulness or nice inspection, even if the age and character of the members of the institution should not render every thing of the kind needless.

Specific Objects to Be Accomplished

1. To increase the number of well-qualified female teachers. The present want of such teachers is well known to all particularly engaged in the cause of education. This deficiency is the occasion of placing many of our schools under the care of those who are not competent to the undertaking.

2. To induce many who have already become teachers, to make further improvement in their education. This institution will furnish such ladies with a full course of instruction, and with society adapted to their age and character, and will give them a more suitable and pleasant home than can now be found connected with any of our female seminaries.

3. To exert an influence in bringing as much of the labor of instruction into the hands of ladies as propriety will admit. This seems important, on account of the many public demands on the time of benevolent, edu-

cated gentlemen, and the comparatively few demands on the time of benevolent, educated ladies.

4. To lead the way toward the establishment of permanent female seminaries in our land. That there are no female seminaries of this character is, we believe, a fact. Those which appear to have the strongest claim to such a standing are so dependent on their present teachers, and their funds and accommodations are to such an extent the property of private individuals, that it would not be safe to predict even their existence the next century.

MOUNT HOLYOKE FEMALE SEMINARY [1]

The selection which follows was written in 1835, during the high point of Miss Lyon's struggle to secure funds for her projected seminary, and although privately printed was never published. The writer stresses the breadth and nobility of the plans of those "benevolent men" who are aiding in the foundation of a seminary to meet a great public need—not a "private want." It is clear that Miss Lyon wishes to draw to her institution young women desirous of "serving their generation," not those "who are wrapped up in self." In referring to the high "literary standard" which it is proposed to maintain at Mount Holyoke, Miss Lyon admits that such a term is indefinite and seeks to give it meaning by declaring that the intellectual culture at Mount Holyoke during its first years will be the same as in the famous seminaries at Ipswich, at Hartford under Catherine Beecher, and at Troy under Emma Willard. However,

[1] The author is indebted to Mount Holyoke College for permission to print this unpublished pamphlet.

she makes it clear that she contemplates "a continued advancement" of standards. The course of study at Ipswich is given in detail and may be compared with the curriculum at Mount Holyoke in 1838–9 (*ante,* pp. 244–245). Miss Lyon's earnest exhortations to future candidates for admission to prepare themselves thoroughly in the fundamental branches was no doubt much needed at that time.

The character of the young ladies, who shall become members of this Seminary the first year, will be of great importance to the prosperity of the Institution itself, and to the cause of female education. Those, who use their influence in making out the number, will sustain no unimportant responsibility. It is very desirable, that the friends of this cause should carefully consider the real design of founding this Institution, before they use their influence to induce any of their friends and acquaintances to avail themselves of its priviliges [*sic.*].

This institution is to be founded by the combined liberality of an enlarged benevolence, which seeks the greatest good on an extensive scale. Some minds seem to be cast in that peculiar mould, that the heart can be drawn forth only by individual want. Others seem best fitted for promoting public good. None can value too much the angel of mercy, that can fly as on the wings of the wind to the individual cry for help as it comes over in tender and melting strains. But who does not venerate those great souls—great by nature—great by education— or great by grace—or by all combined, whose plans and works of mercy are like a broad river swallowing up a thousand little rivulets. How do we stand in awe, when we look down, as on a map, upon their broad and noble plans, destined to give untold blessings to the great community in which they dwell—to their nation—to the world. As we see them urging their way forward, intent on advancing as fast as possible, the renovation of the whole human family—and on hastening the accomplishment of the glorious promises found on the page of inspiration, we are sometimes tempted to draw back their hand, and extend it forth in behalf of some traveller by the wayside, who seems to be overlooked. But we look again, and we behold the dearest personal interests of the traveller by the wayside, and those of a thousand other individuals, included in their large and warm embrace.

This is the class of benevolent men who will aid in founding this Seminary; these the men who are now contributing of their time and money to carry forward this enterprise.

It is ever considered a principle of sacred justice in the management of funds, to regard the wishes of the donors. The great object of those, who are enlisting in this cause, and contributing to it, as to the sacred treasury of the Lord, cannot be misunderstood. It is to meet public and not private wants. They value not individual good less, but the public good more. They have not been prompted to engage in this momentous work by a desire to provide for the wants of a few of the daughters of our land for their own sakes as individuals, but by a desire to provide for the urgent necessities of our country, and of the world, by enlisting in the great work of benevolence, the talents of many of our daughters of fairest promise. This Institution is expected to draw forth the talents of such, to give them a new direction, and to enlist them permanently in the cause of benevolence. We consider it as no more than a due regard to justice, to desire and pray, that a kind Providence may send as scholars to this Seminary, those who shall go forth, and by their deeds, do honor to the Institution, and to the wisdom and benevolence of its founders. The love of justice will also lead us to desire and pray, that the same kind Providence may turn away the feet of those, who may in after life dishonor the Institution, or be simply harmless cumberers of the ground, though they should be our dearest friends, and those who for their own personal benefit, need its privileges more than almost any others.

The grand features of this Institution are to be an elevated standard of science, literature, and refinement, and a moderate standard of expense; all to be guided and modified by the spirit of the gospel. Here we trust will be found a delightful spot for those, "whose heart has stirred them up" to use all their talents in the great work of serving their generation, and of advancing the Redeemer's kingdom.

In the same manner, we doubt not, that the atmosphere will be rendered uncongenial to those who are wrapped up in self, preparing simply to please, and to be pleased, whose highest ambition is, to be qualified to amuse a friend in a vacant hour.

The age of the scholars will aid in giving to the Institution a choice selection of pupils. This Seminary is to be for adult young ladies; at an age when they are called upon by their parents to judge for themselves to a very great degree, and when they can select a spot congenial to their taste. The great and ruling principle—an ardent desire to do the greatest possible good, will we hope, be the presiding spirit in many hearts, bringing together congenial souls. Like many institutions of charity, this does not hold out the prospect of providing for the personal relief of individual sufferers, nor for the direct instruction of the ignorant and degraded. But it does expect to collect, as in a focus, the sparks of benevolence, which are scattered in the hearts of many of our daughters, and after having multiplied them many fold, and having kindled them to a flame, and given them a right direction, to send them out to warm and to cheer the world. Some of them may be the daughters of wealth, and the offering will be no less acceptable, because they have something besides themselves to offer to the great work. Others, may be the daughters of mere competency, having been fitted for the service by an answer to Agur's petition. Others, again may struggle under the pressure of more moderate means, being called to surmount the greatest obstacles by persevering effort, and the aid of friends. But provided they have kindred spirits on the great essential principles, all can go forward together without a discordant note.

It has been stated, that the literary standard of this Institution will be high. This is a very indefinite term. There is no acknowledged standard of female education, by which an institution can be measured. A long list of branches to be taught, can be no standard at all. For if so, a contemplated manual labor school to be established in one of the less improved of the western states, whose prospectus we chanced to notice some two or three years since, would stand higher than most of our New England colleges. Whether the institution was ever established we know not, nor do we remember its name or exact location. But the list of branches to be taught as they appeared on paper, we do remember, as for the time, it served as a happy illustration of a general principle, relating to some of our attempts to advance the cause of education among us. In a seminary for females, we cannot as in the standard of education for the other sex, refer to established institutions, whose course of study and standard of mental discipline are known to every literary man in the land. But it is believed, that our statement cannot be made more intelligible to the enlightened community, than by simply saying, that the course of study, and standard of mental culture will be the same as that of the Hartford Female Seminary— of the Ipswich Female Seminary—or of the Troy Female Seminary—or of some other institution that has stood as long, and ranked as high as these seminaries. Suffice it to say, that it is expected, that the Mount Holyoke Female Seminary will take the Ipswich Female Seminary for its literary standard. Of course there will be room for a continued advancement; as that institution has been raising its own standard from year to year. But at the commencement, the standard is to be as high as the present standard of that seminary. It is to adopt the same high standard of mental discipline—the same slow, thorough, and patient manner of study; the same systematic and extensive course of solid branches. Though this explanation will not be universally understood, yet it is believed that it will be understood by a great many in New England, and by many out of New England—by those, who have long been intimately acquainted with the character of that seminary, or who have witnessed its fruits in the lives of those whom it has sent forth to exert a power over society, which cannot be exerted by mere goodness, without intellectual strength. "By their fruits ye shall know them."

The following is an extract from the last catalogue of the Ipswich Female Seminary.

Course of Study, &c. [At Ipswich]

The regular course will consist of primary studies, and a two years' course in the regular classes, denominated Junior and Senior.

It is not expected that all who enter the school, will pursue the regular course. Those among the more advanced pupils, who design to continue members of the school no more than one year, may either pursue an outline of the branches here taught, or make it an object to gain a thorough knowledge of such studies as seem best suited to promote their individual improvement. In recitations, the regular classes are not kept distinct; but all the pupils are arranged in temporary classes as may best promote the good of individuals.

MARY LYON

PRIMARY STUDIES

Mental Arithmetic,
Written Arithmetic,
English Grammar,
First Book of Euclid's Geometry,
Modern and Ancient Geography,
Government of the United States,
Modern and Ancient History,
Botany,
Watts on the Mind.

STUDIES OF THE JUNIOR CLASS

Written Arithmetic completed,
English Grammar continued,
The Second, Third, and Fourth Books of Euclid's Geometry,
Natural Philosophy,
Chemistry,
Astronomy,
Intellectual Philosophy,
Rhetoric.

STUDIES OF THE SENIOR CLASS

Some of the preceding studies reviewed and continued,
Algebra,
Ecclesiastical History,
Natural Theology,
Philosophy of Natural History,
Analogy of Natural and Revealed Religion to the Constitution
   and Laws of Nature.
Evidences of Christianity.

Reading, Composition, Calisthenics, Vocal Music, the
Bible and several of the above branches of study, will

receive attention through the course. Those who are deficient in spelling and writing, will have exercises in these branches whatever may be their other attainments. Linear drawing will also receive attention. It is desired, that so far as practicable, young ladies before entering the Seminary, should be skilful in both mental and written Arithmetic, and thoroughly acquainted with Geography and the History of the United States.

In order that this new institution may accomplish the greatest good to the cause of female education, it is desirable that the pupils should advance as far as possible in study before entering the Seminary. To many who are expecting to become members, it is a subject of deep regret that the commencement of operations should be delayed so long. To all, who are expecting to enter this seminary when it opens, it is earnestly recommended to spend as much of the intermediate time as possible in study. It is very desirable that the *least* improved of the pupils should have a thorough knowledge of arithmetic, geography, history of the United States and English grammar, though this may not be rigidly required of every individual the first year. These branches may be pursued privately without a regular teacher, or in the common district school, or in the young ladies' village school, or in any other situation, which may be convenient.

Those who wish to pursue these branches without a regular teacher to direct them, may derive advantage by pursuing something like the following order of study.

1. Colburn's First Lessons to the 11th Section;
2. A general course of Geography;
3. Adams' New Arithmetic to Fractions;
4. Rudiments and general principles of English Grammar;
5. Colburn's First Lessons completed;
6. Adams' Arithmetic to Proportion;
7. History of the United States;
8. Thorough course of Geography;
9. Thorough course of English Grammar;
10. Adams' Arithmetic completed.

MANNER OF STUDYING

Colburn's First Lessons

This book should be studied through so many times, and with such close attention, that all the difficult questions in every part of the book can be solved with great readiness, and the manner of solution described. In studying this, recitations are very important. In recitations the book should not be opened by the learner. If the questions cannot be remembered, and all parts comprehended, as they are received from the lips of a teacher, it may be safely inferred, not that there is any deficiency in the ability of the learner, but that more hard study is still requisite. If a young lady attempts to gain a thorough knowledge of this book by private study at home, it is important for her to recite daily to a brother, or sister, or some other friend. In recitations whether of a class, or of an individual, every answer, and every description should be given with great clearness, accuracy, and promptness. The effects of a continued practice of reciting in this way, both on the mind, and degree of intelligence in the manner of an individual, can rarely be realized by those unaccustomed to observe them.

Adams's New Arithmetic

(Some other book may be used as a substitute.)

In pursuing this branch of study, two things should be gained.

1. *Perfect Accuracy.* It should not be considered sufficient, that a question is finally solved correctly. No standard of accuracy is high enough, except that which will enable the learner to avoid all wrong steps in the statement, and all errors in every part of the process to be corrected by a second trial. Where a deficiency is observed in these respects, more close and careful study should be applied—the preceding parts of the book should be slowly and carefully reviewed—and every question should be solved the first time very slowly,

and with an undivided attention, till accurate habits are acquired.

2. *Readiness and Rapidity*. These habits can be gained only by abundant practice. Reciting, that is, solving questions given out by another, will be very useful. This study may be pursued without a regular teacher, but the learner should recite daily to some friend as recommended in Colburn's First Lessons. If any one is under the necessity of being her own teacher, of solving her own questions, and of overcoming her own difficulties, she will receive aid from observing the following rule. "Whenever you are involved in difficulties, from which you know not how to extricate yourself, go back to the beginning, or nearly to the beginning of the book, and solve every question in course till you come to the point of difficulty."

Most individuals will probably find it necessary to go through the whole book two or three times, in order to gain the needful accuracy and readiness.

English Grammar

But few succeed in studying this except with a regular teacher. Though the manner of pursuing this branch is very important, it is not easy to give short and specific directions. We will only say, Be very thorough. Study every lesson closely and carefully.

Geography

The manner of studying this branch must depend much on the teacher. One direction may be given for the use of those who study it without a teacher. After studying regularly through some book, and reviewing it carefully once or twice, let the learner select a complete outline, embracing prominent facts relating to every part of the world. This outline should be reviewed weekly or monthly for months, or for a year or two, till the facts are so indelibly fixed on the memory, that the lady at any future time of life, could recal [*sic*] anything in this outline almost as readily as she could recollect the order of the letters of the alphabet. The learner is referred to a lecture delivered before the American Institute in 1833.

History of the United States

In studying history, some systematic method is very important. But very little dependence can be placed on mere reading. Here and there a mind can be found, which will by a regular reading of history, select and arrange its materials so systematically, that they can be laid up for future use. But such minds among young ladies in the present state of female education are rarely found. History furnishes to the teacher an almost boundless field for the exercise of the inventive powers. But the most successful parts of almost every system of teaching history, cannot be so described as to be used by a young lady without a teacher. An intelligent young lady might use the "Topic System" as it has been called to considerable advantage in the following manner. After gaining a general view of the book to be studied, let the young lady select a list of topics or subjects through the whole, to be learned and recited to some friend, like a connected narration. In learning these topics, it would not be well to charge the memory with every item which can be found, but with those which are the most important. In reciting, she should not attempt to state anything, of which she is not confident, but in what she does attempt to communicate, she should not allow herself the least indulgence for inaccuracy. She should charge herself with deficiency for the least inaccurate statement, even though she should correct it the next moment. The list of topics might with profit be recited through two or three times. If Goodrich's History of the United States is studied, Emerson's Questions may be used with advantage in connexion with the topics. Any one not accustomed to recite by the topic system, might use the Questions as a general guide in selecting items under each topic. Beginners have often found it useful in a few of the first lessons, to write out the items under each topic. But very soon, the mind will be able to collect and arrange its materials without consuming so much time. When topics are written, no use should be made of the notes during recitations.

If the whole of this course cannot be completed before entering the Seminary, let the first part be taken in order, and let what is done, be done thoroughly. After completing the preceding course in the manner described, young ladies can select for themselves from the regular course of study pursued at Ipswich. It is desirable to advance in study as far as possible before entering the seminary, provided that every branch taken up receives thorough attention. A superficial passing over any branch before commencing it regularly in school, is always an injury instead of a benefit. But the greater the real capital, which any one possesses of improvement on entering the institution, the greater will be her proportionate income. Any who hope to be so far advanced as to enter the Senior Class at first, and complete the regular course of study in one year, may need some more specific directions and information relative to preparatory studies, to prevent disappointment. Such can obtain further information by directing a letter to Miss Mary Lyon, South Hadley, Mass. A thorough knowledge of a definite number of branches, is a term, which to different individuals has very different meanings. Some of the members of the Ipswich Female Seminary, who had gone through the regular course, except the studies of the Senior Class, have been successful teachers in some of the most important female seminaries in our country. The same high standard will be taken in this institution. But notwithstanding this, a few individuals, who are now making their arrangements with reference to a hope, that they shall be its members the first year, can be prepared to complete the course, and others there doubtless will be, who could do it by devoting all the time that they can command, before the institution commences, to pursuing the most important studies, and to reviewing those which they have gone over.

This institution will do much, we hope, to raise among the female part of the community a higher standard of science and literature—of economy and of refinement—of benevolence and religion. To accomplish this great end, we hope by the influence of the institution on the community, to lead many to discover and use the means within their reach, instead of mourning in indolence after those they can never enjoy. We hope to redeem from waste a great amount of precious time—of noble intellect, and of moral power.

This was written for the benefit of those, who are making inquiries about the qualifications for admission into this Seminary. It has been printed to save the labor of transcribing. Those into whose hands it may fall, are requested to make no other use of it than they would of a written communication.

M. L.

South Hadley, Sept. 1835.

PRINCIPLES AND DESIGN OF THE MOUNT HOLYOKE FEMALE SEMINARY [1]

Five years after the publication of her first appeal, Miss Lyon wrote a description of the "Principles and Design" of the seminary but recently completed (1837). In this full exposition the reader may perceive the greater definiteness and scope which the plan has taken on as it germinated in the author's mind. Although the principal design of the seminary is to prepare teachers, it will also fit women for "other spheres of usefulness." The writer disclaims any intention that the new seminary shall serve purely local need or private interest; it "is designed entirely for the public good." Again the permanent character of the institution is stressed, founded as it is on a sound economic basis by means of the "sacred charities" of thousands of donors. Miss Lyon makes an appeal to "public benevolence" to carry on the project but just begun and thus permit of its enlargement. Already she is contemplating a seminary

[1] From Hitchcock, Edward, op. cit., pp. 295–308.

of greater size and wider influence. The religious spirit which permeates the article is noteworthy, especially the reference to the "salvation of the world" which the seminary is to assist in carrying forward. In her discussion of "Physical Culture" Miss Lyon is far more conservative than Catherine Beecher and, indeed, admits that her seminary "professes to make no remarkable physical renovations."

————

This institution is established at South Hadley, Massachusetts. It is to be principally devoted to the preparing of female teachers. At the same time, it will qualify ladies for other spheres of usefulness. The design is to give a solid, extensive, and well-balanced English education, connected with that general improvement, that moral culture, and those enlarged views of duty, which will prepare ladies to be educators of children and youth, rather than to fit them to be mere teachers, as the term has been technically applied. Such an education is needed by every female who takes the charge of a school, and sustains the responsibility of guiding the whole course and of forming the entire character of those committed to her care. And when she has done with the business of teaching in a regular school, she will not give up her profession; she will still need the same well-balanced education at the head of her own family and in guiding her own household.

1. This institution professes to be founded on the high principle of enlarged Christian benevolence. In its plans and in its appeals it seeks no support from local or private interest. It is designed entirely for the public good, and the trustees would adopt no measures not in accordance with this design. It is sacredly consecrated to the great Head of the church, and they would not seek for human approbation by any means which will not be well pleasing in his sight.

2. The institution is designed to be permanent. The permanency of an institution may be considered as consisting of two particulars—first, its perpetual vitality, and second, its continual prosperity and usefulness. The first is to be secured in the same manner that the principle of perpetual life in our higher institutions for young men has been so effectually preserved. A fund is to be committed to an independent, self-perpetuating board of trustees, known to the churches as faithful, responsible men; not as a proprietary investment, but as a free offering, leaving them no way for an honorable retreat from their trust, and binding them with solemn responsibilities to hundreds and thousands of donors, who have committed their sacred charities to

their conscientious fidelity. Give to a literary institution, on this principle, an amount of property sufficient to be viewed as an object of great importance, and it is almost impossible to extinguish its vital life by means of adversity. How firmly have our colleges stood amidst the clashing elements around us, and the continual over-turnings which are taking place in the midst of us!

The usefulness of this institution, like all others, must depend on its character. This may be very good for a time, where there is no principle of perpetual life, as is the case with some of our most distinguished female seminaries. Amidst all their prosperity, they have no solid foundation, and in themselves no sure principle of continued existence. Could we secure to our public in-stitutions the continued labors of the same teachers through an antediluvial life, the preservation of the vital principle would be a subject of much less consequence. But in view of the present shortened life of man, ren-dered shorter still by disease and premature decay, and in view of the many changes which are ever breaking in upon the continued services of those to whose care these institutions are committed, every reflecting mind must regard it as of the very first importance to secure to them this principle, especially to a public seminary for the raising up of female teachers.

3. The institution is to be entirely for an older class

of young ladies. The general system for family arrangements, for social improvement, for the division of time, for organizing and regulating the school, and the requirements for entrance, will be adapted throughout to young ladies of adult age and of mature character. Any provision in an institution like this for younger misses must be a public loss far greater than the individual good. Their exclusion from the institution will produce a state of society among the members exceedingly pleasant and profitable to those whose great desire is to be prepared to use all their talents in behalf of the cause of education, and of the Redeemer's kingdom; and it will secure for their improvement the entire labors of the teachers, without an interruption from the care and government of pupils too immature to take care of themselves.

4. The young ladies are to take a part in the domestic work of the family. This also is to be on the principle of equality. All are to take part, not as a servile labor, for which they are to receive a small weekly remuneration, but as a gratuitous service to the institution of which they are members, designed for its improvement and elevation. The first object of this arrangement is, to give to the institution a greater degree of independence. The arrangements for boarding all the pupils in the establishment will give to us an independence with

regard to private families in the neighborhood, without which it would be difficult, if not impossible, to secure its perpetual prosperity. The arrangements for the domestic work will, in a great measure, relieve it from another source of depressing dependence—a dependence on the will of hired domestics, to which many a family in New England is subject.

The other object of this arrangement is to promote the health, the improvement, and the happiness of the pupils; their health, by its furnishing them with a little daily exercise of the best kind; their improvement, by its tending to preserve their interest in domestic pursuits; and their happiness, by its relieving them from that servile dependence on common domestics, to which young ladies, as mere boarders in a large establishment, are often subject, to their great inconvenience. The adoption of a feature like this, in an institution which aims to be better endowed than any other existing female seminary in the country, must give it an attitude of noble independence, which can scarcely fail to exert an elevating influence on its members.

This cause is the humble, but firm and efficient patron of all other branches of benevolence. What the present generation is beginning to accomplish for the salvation of the world it seeks to preserve and carry forward with increasing rapidity. Whatever of conquest is now gained it seeks to secure forever from the encroachments of the enemy. It seeks to lay the foundation strong, on which, under God, the temple, with all its increasing weight, is to rise, and be sustained, and to secure it from injury and decay. It looks abroad on a world lying in wickedness. It beholds with painful interest the slow progress of these United States in carrying the blessings of salvation to the two hundred millions, who are the estimated proportion of the inhabitants of this benighted world to be converted to God through our instrumentality. And as it attempts in vain to calculate the time when the work shall be accomplished, it would fain increase its progress a hundred fold, by training up the children in the way they should go. It has endeavored to fix an eye on the distant point of futurity, when, according to a fair and reasonable computation, this nation, with all its increasing millions, and the inhabitants of the whole earth, shall be supplied with faithful, educated ministers of the gospel. And as it inquires, in vain, "When shall these things be?" and as it attempts, in vain, to count up the millions on millions who shall go down to everlasting death before that time *can* arrive, it would fain strive, with unparalleled efforts, through the children of our country, greatly to multiply the number of ministers during the next generation, and to carry forward the work in an unexampled and increasing ratio through the generations which shall follow.

The object of this institution penetrates too far into futurity, and takes in too broad a view, to discover its claims to the passing multitude. We appeal in its behalf to wise men, who can judge what we say. We appeal to those who can venture as pioneers in the great work of renovating a world. Others may stand waiting for the great multitude to go forward, but then is the time when these men feel themselves called upon to make their greatest efforts, and to do their noblest deeds of benevolence. Thus we hope it will be in behalf of this institution.

We commend this enterprise to the continued prayers and efforts of its particular friends, of all those who have enlisted in its behalf, and have given of their time, their influence, and their substance. We would invite them to come with us around the same sacred altar, and there consecrate this beloved institution, as first fruits, to the Lord, to be devoted forever to his service.

This enterprise, thus far, has been under the care of a kind Providence. It has not been carried forward by might, nor by power; but in every step of its progress the good hand of God has been upon it. Let all its friends bring in the tithes and the offerings, and let them commit the disposing of the whole to Him who can accomplish the work which his own hands have commenced, and he will pour out upon this institution, and the cause with which it is connected, and upon the children and youth of our country, and of the world, a blessing, that there shall not be room enough to receive it.

TENDENCIES OF THE PRINCIPLES EMBRACED AND THE SYSTEM ADOPTED IN THE MOUNT HOLYOKE FEMALE SEMINARY

The enterprise of founding this seminary was commenced nearly five years ago. More than three years were occupied in preparing the way, in raising the funds, and in erecting the building now occupied. It was ready for the reception of scholars November 8, 1837.

The original plan was to provide for two hundred. Only the first building has yet been erected. This can accommodate only ninety. Though it is a noble edifice, and well adapted to its end, it is but a beginning. Full one half of the funds must yet be raised. In order to finish the plan, at least twenty thousand dollars more will be needed for the buildings, besides perhaps five thousand dollars or more for furniture, library, and apparatus.

This seminary is specific in its character, and, of

course, does not provide for the entire education of a young lady. Such a provision may be found expedient in foreign countries, where all systems can be brought under the rigid rules of monarchy, without being subject to the continual encroachments and changes necessarily resulting from a free government. But in our country it is doubted whether female seminaries generally can attain a high standard of excellence till they become more specific and less mixed in their character.

1. *Religious Culture.* This lies at the foundation of that female character which the founders of this seminary have contemplated. Without this, their efforts would entirely fail of their design. This institution has been for the Lord, that it might be peculiarly his own. It has been solemnly and publicly dedicated to his service. It has been embalmed by prayer in many hearts, and consecrated around many a family altar. The donors and benefactors of this institution, with its trustees and teachers, have felt a united obligation to seek, in behalf of this beloved seminary, "first the kingdom of God and his righteousness." Endeavors have been made to raise the funds and to lay the whole foundation on Christian principles, to organize a school and form a family that from day to day might illustrate the precepts and spirit of the gospel. Public worship, the Bible lesson, and other appropriate duties of the Sabbath, a

regular observance of secret devotion, suitable attention to religious instruction and social prayer meetings, and the maintaining of a consistent Christian deportment, are considered the most important objects of regard, for both teachers and scholars. The friends of this seminary have sought that this might be a spot where souls shall be born of God, and where much shall be done for maturing and elevating Christian character. The smiles of Providence and the influences of the Holy Spirit have encouraged them to hope that their desires will not be in vain.

2. *Cultivation of Benevolence.* This is implied in the last particular, but it needs special care in a lady's education. While many of the present active generation are fixed in their habits, and will never rise above the standard of benevolence already adopted, the eye of hope rests with anxious solicitude on the next generation. But who shall take all the little ones, and by precept, and still more by example, enforce on them the sentiments of benevolence, and, aided by the Holy Spirit, train them up from their infancy for the service of the Redeemer? Is there not here an appropriate sphere for the efforts of women, through whose moulding hands all our children and youth must inevitably pass?

How important, then, is it that the education of a female should be conducted on strictly benevolent principles! and how important that this spirit should be the presiding genius in every female school! Should it not be so incorporated with its nature, and so wrought into its very existence, that it cannot prosper without it? Such a school the friends of this seminary have sought to furnish. They would have the spirit of benevolence manifest in all its principles, and in the manner of conferring its privileges, in the mutual duties it requires of its members, and in the claims it makes on them to devote their future lives to doing good.

3. *Intellectual Culture.* This trait of character is of inestimable value to a lady who desires to be useful. A thorough and well-balanced intellectual education will be to her a valuable auxiliary in every department of duty.

This seminary has peculiar advantages for gaining a high intellectual standard. The age required for admission will secure to the pupils, as a whole, greater mental power, and the attainments required for admission will secure to the institution a higher standard of scholarship.

4. *Physical Culture.* The value of health to a lady is inestimable. Her appropriate duties are so numerous and varied, and so constant in their demands, and so imperious in the moment of their calls, as will render this treasure to her above price. How difficult is it for

her to perform all her duties faithfully and successfully, unless she possesses at all times a calm mind, an even temper, a cheerful heart, and a happy face! But a feeble system and a nervous frame are often the direct antagonists of these indispensable traits in a lady's character. A gentleman may possibly live and do some good without much health; but what can a lady do, unless she takes the attitude of an invalid, and seeks to do good principally by patience and submission? If a gentleman cannot do his work in one hour, he may perhaps do it in another; but a lady's duties often allow of no compromise in hours. If a gentleman is annoyed and vexed with the nervousness of his feeble frame, he may perhaps use it to some advantage, as he attempts to move the world by his pen, or by his voice. But a lady cannot make such a use of this infirmity in her influence over her children and family—an influence which must be all times under the control of gentleness and equanimity. Much has been said on this subject, but enough has not been *done,* in our systems of education, to promote the health of young ladies. This is an object of special regard in this seminary.

The time is all regularly and systematically divided. The hours for rising and retiring are early. The food is plain and simple, but well prepared, and from the best materials. No article of second quality of the *kind* is ever purchased for the family, and no standard of cooking is allowed but that of doing every thing as well as it can be done. The day is so divided that the lessons can be well learned, and ample time allowed for sleep; the hour for exercise in the domestic department can be secured without interruption, and a half hour in the morning and evening for secret devotion, also half an hour for vocal music, and twenty minutes for calisthenics. Besides, there are the leisure hours, in which much is done of sewing, knitting, and ornamental needlework; and much is enjoyed in social intercourse, in walking, and in botanical excursions. This institution presupposes a good degree of health and correct habits. But little can be done in this seminary, or any other, for those whose constitution is already impaired, or whose physical habits, up to the age of sixteen, are particularly defective. This institution professes to make no remarkable physical renovations. But it is believed that a young lady who is fitted for the system, and who can voluntarily and cheerfully adopt it as her own, will find this place favorable for preserving unimpaired the health she brings with her, and for promoting and establishing the good physical habits already acquired.

5. *Social and Domestic Character.* The excellence of the female character in this respect consists principally in a preparation to be happy herself in her social and

domestic relations, and to make all others happy around her. All her duties, of whatever kind, are in an important sense social and domestic. They are retired and private and not public, like those of the other sex. Whatever she does beyond her own family should be but another application and illustration of social and domestic excellence. She may occupy the place of an important teacher, but her most vigorous labors should be modest and unobtrusive. She may go on a foreign mission, but she will there find a retired spot, where, away from the public gaze, she may wear out or lay down a valuable life. She may promote the interests of the Sabbath school, or be an angel of mercy to the poor and afflicted; she may seek in various ways to increase the spirit of benevolence and the zeal for the cause of missions; and she may labor for the salvation of souls; but her work is to be done by the whisper of her still and gentle voice, by the silent step of her unwearied feet, and by the power of her uniform and consistent example.

The following elements should be embraced in the social and domestic character of a lady:

(a) *Economy*. Economy consists in providing well at little comparative expense. It necessarily implies good judgment and good taste. It can be equally manifested in the tasteful decorations of a palace and in the simple comforts of a cottage. Suppose all ladies possessed this in a high degree, how much more would be found in families of comfort and convenience, of taste and refinement, of education and improvement, of charity and good works!

This institution, it is well known, is distinguished for its economical features. Economy, however, is not adopted principally for its own sake, but as a means of education, as a mode of producing favorable effects on character, and of preparing young ladies for the duties of life. The great object is to make the school really better. An economical character is to be formed by precept, by practice, and by example. Example has great effect, not only in furnishing a model for imitation, but also in proving that economy is practicable, which is one of the most essential requisites for success. Let a young lady spend two or three years, on intimate terms, in a family distinguished for a judicious and consistent illustration of this principle, and the effects cannot be lost.

(b) *A Suitable Feeling of Independence.* There are two kinds of dependence, very unlike in their nature, but both inconsistent with the highest degree of domestic bliss. To one of these ladies in cities and large towns are more particularly subject; but it is an evil from which ladies in the country are not wholly ex-

empt. It is a feeling of dependence on the will of servants. Every lady should be so educated, as far as it can
be done, that she will feel able to take care of herself,
and, if need be, of a family, whatever may be her situation in life, and whatever her station in society. Otherwise, if she remains in these United States, she may be
rendered unhappy by constantly feeling that her daily
comforts are at the control of her servants, who in such
cases are often unfaithful, unreasonable, and dissatis-
fied. The withering effects of family perplexities on the
social character is well known to every observer of domestic life. On the other hand, how much happiness
often results from a suitable feeling of independence.
A lady in one of our large cities, who is distinguished
for having faithful servants, considers the secret as lying
in her feeling of independence. If one, in a fit of caprice,
proposes leaving her, she has only to say, "You may go
to-day. If need be, I can take care of my own family
until your place is supplied."

Against this kind of dependence this institution seeks
to exert its decided influence. The whole aspect of the
family, and all the plans of the school, are suited to cultivate habits entirely the reverse. In the domestic independence of the household all have an interest. The
daily hour for these duties returns to each at the appointed time, and no one inquires whether it can be

omitted or transferred to another. No one receives any pecuniary reward for her services, and no one seeks with her money to deprive herself of the privilege of sharing in the freedom, simplicity, and independence of her *home*.

There is another kind of independence entirely different in its nature, but equally essential to a high degree of domestic happiness. This is the result of economy already considered. It is the power of bringing personal and family expenses fairly and easily within the means enjoyed. The whole system adopted in this seminary is designed to give a living illustration of the principle by which this power is to be gained. This ability will be of immense value in active life. It will prepare one to sustain the reverses of fortune with submission, or to meet the claims of hospitality and charity with promptness. This kind of independence might be to the great cause of benevolence like an overflowing fountain, whose streams will never fail.

(c) *Skill and Expedition in Household Duties.* Let a young lady despise this branch of the duties of woman, and she despises the appointments of the Author of her existence. The laws of God, made known by nature and by providence, and also by the Bible, enjoin these duties on the sex, and she cannot violate them with impunity. Let her have occasion to preside at the head of her own family and table, and she may despair of enjoying herself, or of giving to others the highest degree of domestic happiness. Does she seek to do good by teaching? The time, we hope, is not far distant, when no mother will commit her daughters to the influence of such a teacher. Does she seek to do good in the Sabbath school? How can she enforce all the duties to God and man in their due proportion while she contemns one of the most obvious laws of her nature? Would she endeavor to show the poor and the ignorant how to find the comforts of life? How can she teach what she has never learned? Does she become the wife of a missionary? How does her heart sink within her, as her desponding husband strives in vain to avoid the evils resulting from her inefficiency!

This institution is not designed to conduct this branch of a young lady's education. It would not take this privilege from the mother. But it does seek to preserve the good habits already acquired, and to make a favorable impression with regard to the value of system, promptness, and fidelity in this branch of the duties of woman. . . .

1. *In Furnishing a Supply of Female Teachers*. Teaching is really the business of almost every useful woman. If there are any to whom this does not apply, they may be considered as exceptions to a general rule. Of course,

no female is well educated who has not all the acquisitions necessary for a good teacher. The most essential qualifications are thorough mental culture, a well-balanced character, a benevolent heart, an ability to communicate knowledge and apply it to practice, an acquaintance with human nature, and the power of controlling the minds of others.

But it is not enough that a great number of ladies are well educated. They must also have benevolence enough to engage in teaching, when other duties will allow and when their labors are needed. Female teachers should not expect to be fully compensated for their services, unless it be by kindness and gratitude.

There are many other chords in female hearts which will vibrate much more tenderly and powerfully than this. There is a large and increasing number of educated ladies, who will make the best of teachers, but who can be allured much more by respectful attention, by kindness and gratitude, by suitable school-rooms and apparatus, and other facilities for rendering their labors pleasant and successful, than they can by the prospect of a pecuniary reward.

The spirit of this seminary is suited not only to increase the number of educated ladies, but to enforce on them the obligation to use their talents for the good of others, especially in teaching. It is hoped it may also lead them to be more willing to take any school and in any place where their services are most needed.

2. *In Promoting the Prosperity of Common Schools.* Whoever will devise means by which reading, spelling, arithmetic, geography, and grammar shall receive as thorough attention in common schools as they deserve, and whoever will throw inducements before the older female scholars to remain in them longer and attend thoroughly to these branches, as an example to others, will do much to elevate their standard. Such an influence this seminary seeks to exert.

3. *In Counteracting Certain Errors Which Have Prevailed to Some Extent in Female Education.*

First Error. Tasking the mind too early with severe mental discipline.—The evils of this course are beginning to be felt by careful observers of the human mind and of human character. When the effort is attended with the greatest success, there is generally the greatest injury. The most discouraging field which any teacher was ever called to cultivate is the mind of a young lady who has been studying all her days, and has gone over most of the natural and moral sciences without any valuable improvement, until she is tired of school, tired of books, and tired almost of life. As this institution proposes to conduct young ladies through a regular intellectual course, after the age of sixteen, its influence will be against this error.

Second Error. Deferring some parts of education till too late a period.—Among the things neglected till too late a period are the manners, the cultivation of the voice, including singing, pronunciation, and all the characteristics of good reading, gaining skill and expedition in the common necessary mechanical operations, such as sewing, knitting, writing, and drawing, and acquiring, by daily practice, a knowledge and a love of domestic pursuits. To these might be added some things which depend almost entirely on the memory, such as spelling, and others which are suited to lay the foundation of a literary taste, such as a judicious course of reading, practice in composition, &c. Those who are to attend to instrumental music, the ornamental branches, and the pronunciation of foreign languages, must commence early.

Third Error. Placing Daughters too young in a Boarding-school or large Seminary.—A common boarding-school is not a suitable place for a little girl. She needs the home of her childhood, or one like it. Direct individual attention, such as can be given by no one who has the care of many, is the necessary means of forming her character, of cultivating her manners, of developing her affections, and of nurturing all that is lovely and of good report. She wants the uninterrupted sympathies of a mother's heart. She needs a constant and gentle hand, leading her singly along in the path of safety and improvement. Perhaps the evils of a boarding-house are most unfavorable on her character just as she is entering her teens. Who can guide this self-sufficient age but the mother, who has gained a permanent place in her affections and a decided influence over her life? Who but the mother, who first taught her to obey, can lay on her the necessary restrictions without exposing her to form the unlovely trait of character gained by complaining of those whom she should love and respect, and who deserve her gratitude?

4. *In giving just Views of the Advantages of large female Seminaries.* Such institutions furnish peculiar privileges, which cannot be secured by smaller schools; but in most cases they have not been able to produce their legitimate results. They have often suffered for the want of accommodations and other facilities for successful operation, from their temporary and unsettled existence, from their want of system, and sometimes from too public a location, and too public an aspect in their features. Their efforts also to accommodate all ages and all classes often prevent their having any fixed or

determinate character. This institution seeks to avoid all these evils, and to develop the real advantages of a large seminary.

In order that a lady may have the most thorough education, she should spend a number of years in close intellectual application after her mental powers have acquired sufficient strength, and her physical system sufficient maturity, and after she has all the necessary preparation. This must be during the best part of her life, when every year is worth more than can be estimated in gold and silver. Facilities for success should be given her, which will be an ample reward for the sacrifice of so much time. Whoever has undertaken to organize a school has had abundant evidence that all these points cannot be gained where the number is not large. This seminary is able now to secure all these advantages in some degree, but not so perfectly as it will when the two hundred can be received.

The influence of a large seminary on the social character is also important. The very discipline necessary to preserve little girls from exposure to injury, and to cultivate the principles of virtue and loveliness, is attended with some necessary evils which will need a pruning hand at a maturer age. Not the least prominent of these is a narrowness of soul, giving her limited views of others.

The spirit of monopolizing privileges is to some extent the effect of giving to a little girl all that individual care and affectionate attention which her cultivation demands. A large seminary, and more especially a large family, have a tendency to remove this. The young lady needs to feel herself a member of a large community, where the interests of others are to be sought equally with her own. She needs to learn by practice, as well as by principle, that individual accommodations and private interests are to be sacrificed for the public good; and she needs to know from experience that those who make such a sacrifice will receive an ample reward in the improvement of the community among whom they are to dwell.

5. *In giving the Claims of large female Seminaries an acknowledged Place among the other Objects of public Benevolence.* The claims of those for the other sex were admitted two hundred years ago; and the colleges, academies, and theological seminaries, all over the land, show that the wise and the good have not been weary in well doing. How ridiculous would be the attempt to found colleges in the manner that some female seminaries have been founded! Suppose a gentleman, having a large family depending on him for support, finds his health not sufficient for the duties of his profession. Casting his eye around, he looks on the office of a presi-

dent of a college as affording more ample means, and a more pleasant and respectable situation for his family, than any other he can command. But a new college must be founded to furnish him the place. He selects a large village in New England, or at the west, or at the south, as may best favor the accomplishment of his object, and where he can find buildings which he can buy or rent on some conditions, though they may be far from being adapted to such an end. He purchases his apparatus, or has none, and procures professors on his own responsibility. Thus prepared, he commences, making his charge to the students such as will meet the rent of buildings, furniture, and apparatus, and the salaries of his professors, besides furnishing a handsome support to his own family. What could such a college do to encourage thorough and systematic education in our country? But this is scarcely a caricature of the manner in which some female seminaries have been founded.

We cannot hope for a state of things essentially better till the principle is admitted that female seminaries, designed for the public benefit, must be founded by the hand of public benevolence, and be subject to the rules enjoined by such benevolence. Let this principle be fully admitted, and let it have sufficient time to produce its natural effects, and it will be productive of more important results than can be easily estimated. Then our large seminaries may be permanent, with all the mutual responsibilities and cooperation which the principle of permanency produces.

INDEX

INDEX

INDEX

INDEX

INDEX